"This book is essential for Christian parents, youth workers, and educators as we seek to draw our children into the difficult conversations surrounding gender identity. Mark Yarhouse provides an incredible way of helping adults understand the topic and gives suggestions for engaging young people in a conversation that cannot be avoided. He also provides a conceptualization of learning together and having conversations that are led by Christian conviction and compassionate civility."

Erik Ellefsen, director of networks and improvement for the School of Education's Center for School Leadership, Baylor University

"This extraordinary book is the most helpful we've read on the topic. Dr. Yarhouse offers learnings from scientific research in civil and compassionate language for Christian parents to have healthy and helpful conversations with their children about gender identity. *Talking to Kids about Gender Identity* is a must-read for Christian parents, ministry leaders, and health care professionals. It will save lives!"

Greg and Lynn McDonald, co-founders of Embracing the Journey, Inc.

"The calm, compassionate, and careful tone of Yarhouse will lessen parents' heightened anxiety and fear around gender identity, As will his practical advice based in both faith and clinical experience. Parents will be relieved to find themselves saying, 'We can do this,' as they anticipate these conversations with their children."

Janet B. Dean, MDiv, PhD, professor of pastoral counselor education, Asbury Theological Seminary

Talking to Kids about

Gender Identity

Books by Mark Yarhouse

Talking to Kids about

Gender Identity

A Roadmap for Christian Compassion,
Civility, and Conviction

MARK YARHOUSE

BETHANYHOUSE
a division of Baker Publishing Group
Minneapolis, Minnesota

Published by Bethany House Publishers
Minneapolis, Minnesota
www.bethanyhouse.com

Bethany House Publishers is a division of
Baker Publishing Group, Grand Rapids, Michigan

Printed in the United States of America

Library of Congress Cataloging-in-Publication Data
Names: Yarhouse, Mark A., author.
Title: Talking to kids about gender identity : a roadmap for Christian compassion, civility, and conviction / Mark Yarhouse.
Description: Minneapolis, Minnesota : Bethany House Publishers, a division of Baker Publishing Group, [2023] | Includes bibliographical references.
Identifiers: LCCN 2023009158 | ISBN 9780764241178 (trade paper) | ISBN 9780764242281 (casebound) | ISBN 9781493443802 (ebook)
Subjects: LCSH: Gender identity—Religious aspects—Christianity. | Sexual orientation—Religious aspects—Christianity. | Parenting—Religious aspects—Christianity. | Child rearing—Religious aspects—Christianity.
Classification: LCC BT708 .Y369 2023 | DDC 241/.664—dc23/eng/20230421
LC record available at https://lccn.loc.gov/2023009158

All names and some recognizable details have been changed to protect the privacy of those whose stories are shared in this book.

Baker Publishing Group publications use paper produced from sustainable forestry practices and post-consumer waste whenever possible.

23 24 25 26 27 28 29   7 6 5 4 3 2 1

Contents

Contents

Part 4: For the Person Experiencing Gender-Identity Issues

Why This Book Is Important

A few years ago, I was meeting with a mother of a middle school student. She was remarking that she doesn't recall when she first heard about people being transgender; maybe it was around the time of Caitlyn Jenner's transitioning, but no, she did have a vague recollection of knowing about it prior to then but not giving it a lot of thought. When her middle schooler came home one day and mentioned a friend who was trans, she realized she hadn't had any kind of conversation with her son that would help him navigate these concepts in a culture and peer group in which such gender experiences and gender identities are increasingly normal, almost commonplace.[1]

This is a book for Christian parents who are struggling with what to think about gender identity, transgender experiences, and emerging gender identities—and with how to talk to their children about these issues. It is a book for Christian parents figuring out how to respond to the self-descriptions of their children or their children's peers, from "I have gender dysphoria" to "I am gender diverse."

Parents are asking good questions and need reliable resources. You need answers for yourself and, by extension, for your children. You may not feel you have the language to talk about these issues and are not sure what approach to take when discussing them with your children.

Part of the challenge is that you may feel you have few role models for how to think about and engage the topic of gender identity. Because the topic is so polarizing, most parents have access to people on one of two extremes: the "culture warrior"—i.e., the person whose greatest concern is to win a war against ideas they view as threatening to Christianity, and the "cultural capitulator"—i.e., the person whose Christian worldview seems to have no bearing on the topics of sexuality and gender. This person just takes everything in stride, never appearing to critically evaluate shifts in language and categories for gender identity and expression that are used in the broader culture today.

The book you are holding is intended to provide you, parents, with another angle of entry into the conversations you might have with your children about gender identity. Think of yourself as a "cultural ambassador," a person who draws upon their Christian worldview to understand various aspects of God's kingdom. Toward this end, you engage culture with an eye for kingdom considerations.[2] This angle of entry into the conversation should be characterized by "convicted civility seasoned with compassion."[3] Anne Lamott wrote, "You don't always have to chop with the sword of truth. You can point with it too."[4] In other words, the sword of truth doesn't have to be wielded as a weapon, so that you are focused on taking an attacking posture. We can also point with a sword, much as a compass needle points toward true north. Such a maneuver takes you out of both the "capitulator" posture and the "warrior" posture, providing you with a unique opportunity to engage and transform.

As an ambassador, you are open to listening and learning from other people's experiences, as there are people who share your Christian worldview who are navigating gender identity questions, as well as people who do not share your Christian worldview doing the same. As an ambassador, you are also building and maintaining relationships. This is the constant work of a good ambassador. Relationships are maintained over time through a sustained presence. As a Christian, by bringing your sustained presence into the life of another, you make Christ present. You embody the love God has for the person.

My goal is to help you understand how these three Cs (*convicted civility* seasoned with *compassion*) can guide the conversations you have with your kids about gender and gender identity, and their relationships to peers who identify as transgender or who have transitioned.

The book is organized into four parts. The first part of the book provides some basic background information so that you are better positioned to answer your kids' questions and to respond to the teachable moments that are part and parcel of raising kids. We tackle the question of why transgender experiences have suddenly become so prominent (chapter 1), and what causes someone to experience gender dysphoria (chapter 2), which is a condition associated with most transgender experiences. The limited research in this area makes it an especially difficult topic, but I'll go over some of what we know and don't know and how to talk with your kids about it. We then wrestle with what the Bible says about being transgender (chapter 3). This is a crucial topic for Christian parents, and one we want to think through carefully.

The second part of the book moves more deeply into parents' engagement with their children. We'll look at what to tell your child about gender in general (chapter 4). This chapter is part sex education and part affirmation of your child's typical gender experiences (to the degree that your child's experience of gender has been typical so far). We then consider what you could say to your child when they ask you about a classmate who has decided to use a different name and pronouns, to take hormone blockers, or even to pursue a surgical transition (chapter 5). We also address the question of how best to guide your child in their interactions with a transgender friend (chapter 6) who has socially and/or medically transitioned. While chapter 5 is about helping your child understand and respond to a friend's *decision* to transition, chapter 6 is about helping your child respond once the transition has occurred.

In the third part of the book, we want to help parents who are wondering about their own child's experience of gender identity. We'll discuss whether there are any early signs that a child may be struggling with gender dysphoria (chapter 7). How do we distinguish what is in the typical range of gender expression and what takes a child into a different set of considerations, such as the possibility of gender dysphoria? We then consider how you can help your own child if they are struggling with dysphoria (chapter 8).

The final part of the book is for the person who experiences gender dysphoria themselves. *What if this is your story?* We engage this question in chapter 9.

Each chapter will have two special features: Bringing the Conversation Home and Cultural Ambassador: Our Three Cs. Bringing the Conversation Home will illustrate how parents can engage this topic in their own home. In most instances, I'll include dialogue that parents could have with a child or teen. This section is meant to model for you as a Christian parent what is possible and to help you have the words, tone, and posture that will lead to more constructive communication and education.

The other special feature, Cultural Ambassador: Our Three Cs, goes back to what I mentioned above about *convictions*, *civility*, and *compassion*. I want you to think of ways to push beyond the extremes of culture warrior or cultural capitulator. I want to help you engage ideas from the broader culture and "thicken the plot" by bringing Christian considerations into the conversation. Instead of being a culture warrior or cultural capitulator, you can be a cultural ambassador who represents another way of engaging this topic. Because I recommend that parents engage others with *convicted civility seasoned with compassion*, I want these sections to model for you how to apply these three Cs to the topics covered in each chapter.

As a Christian parent, you may be struggling with what to think about transgender experiences, gender dysphoria, and emerging gender identities. If you're like most parents, you're probably also struggling with how to talk to your children about these issues. If so, this book is written specifically for you.

PART 1

The Basics of Gender Identity

1

Why are transgender experiences suddenly so prominent?

Lauren and Daniel[1] came to our clinic for a parent consultation. They wanted to talk about some of the behaviors they were seeing in their son, James, age fourteen. James has been more withdrawn in recent months, but ever since he was four or five, his behavior had Lauren and Daniel asking each other what might be going on. When he was five, James asked his mom if he would grow breasts like she has breasts. Later that same year, James asked Lauren why God gave him a penis. He did not find comfort in his mother's reply: "God made you a boy, and that's why you have a penis. God made you this way, and you are a terrific boy." Other behaviors would follow, as would other statements and questions that Lauren and Daniel found mystifying. When they sat down for the consultation, they noted at one point in the interview that there were at least three other kids at school who identified as transgender, and these were just the kids James knew of. There were likely others. Daniel said, "I've never known a transgender person. This just was not a thing we saw growing up. I don't even know where to begin, to be honest. Why is the transgender issue so huge all of a sudden?"

Parents like Lauren and Daniel are asking, "Why are transgender experiences suddenly so prominent?" What is happening in our culture? Many parents feel like this conversation has come out of the blue in the past few years. You may be feeling the same way and asking the same question: Are more people transgender now—are experiences of gender dysphoria more common than they used to be—or are we just more aware of them?

There are a few ways for us to answer this question.

Are More People Transgender?

Probably the most commonly held view I come across in my field of psychology is that there is no difference in the proportion of people who are transgender today compared with the past—that transgender people have always been here, but what has changed is the social acceptance. Transgender people can now identify themselves openly and publicly, in ways that are new and exciting for them.

But another point of view is that there is a huge increase in the proportion of people who are transgender, and this remarkable increase is the result of social influences such as peer group influence and shared communal identity as a people group. There can be a kind of "social contagion" in which people catch and pass along ways of thinking about themselves, such that they begin to present with similar symptoms to those around them. This is the most commonly held view among critics of some forms of transgender experiences.

Keep in mind that there is a difference between *research* on how common transgender is and *interpretation of research* that seeks to explain why being transgender is more common, if we believe it is. What do the numbers show?

Psychologists in the United States today use a standard manual, called the *Diagnostic and Statistical Manual of Mental Disorders, 5th Edition (DSM-5)*, to diagnose mental disorders. That manual includes a current diagnosis of Gender Dysphoria. Gender Dysphoria refers to the distress associated with gender discordance or lack of fit between a person's gender identity (as a boy or girl, man or woman) and their biological sex (usually thought of in terms of chromosomes, gonads, and genitalia). When a person experiences gender discordance and they find that experience to be distressing, they could meet the criteria for the diagnosis of Gender Dysphoria.

The *DSM-5* says that the percentage of people who have gender dysphoria is remarkably low; it is not a common experience at all.[2] The fine print, however, points out that these estimates are of adults seeking medical interventions from specialty gender clinics in Europe. They aren't good estimates of gender dysphoria among adults in the general population, let alone among children and adolescents. Also, we've seen that most transgender adults don't report using medical interventions[3] such as hormone therapy or various surgical procedures, so those early estimates are very misleading.

If you survey the general populace about their gender identity, you'll find higher estimates of the frequency of people who identify as transgender. Unlike surveying people who go to specialty clinics, surveying people who are just part of the community allows you to include those without sufficient money, time, or interest to pursue specialty services. These surveys can also include people who don't meet the criteria for a formal diagnosis of Gender Dysphoria, and even those who don't experience gender dysphoria at all. If you just survey people and ask them if they are a man or a woman or transgender or a different gender identity, you'll find much higher percentages of transgender experiences reported.[4] It would still be under 1 percent of the population, but that's a lot more than what we thought when we surveyed people going to specialty clinics for medical assistance.

Where the percentages really rise is among younger generations. A recent Gallup Poll indicated that the highest percentages of people saying they are transgender were reported among those in Generation Z, specifically those born between 1997 and 2002. About 2 percent of that group identified as transgender. You get lower percentages among Millennials, who were born between 1981 and 1996, and still lower percentages among Generation X (born between 1965 and 1980) and Baby Boomers (born between 1946 and 1964).[5]

Table 1. Identify as Transgender?

Generation	Years	Percentage
Generation Z	1997–2002	2.1%
Millennials	1981–1996	1.0%
Generation X	1965–1980	0.5%
Baby Boomers	1946–1964	0.1%

I mentioned above that some people view these increases as a result of social contagion. I don't tend to use this phrase—or at least, I don't use it in isolation, as if it alone explains the increases. Sometimes social contagion is offered as an explanation in a way that pits it against the social acceptance theory. It is a very common tendency for people to think in terms of single causes. The single-cause approach allows us to reduce complexity to a simple explanation that is easier to incorporate into our way of making sense of what is going on around us. This is unhelpful. In my mind, there are undoubtedly multiple influences impacting the rise in transgender identification. Social acceptance is certainly going to increase the number of people who are aware of their gender discordance or are willing to acknowledge that discordance and now have a name for it. To the extent that social contagion occurs, it likely occurs for a

What is Social Contagion?

Social contagion refers to "the spread of behaviors, attitudes, and affect through crowds and other types of social [relationships] from one member to another."[6] When we apply this concept to mental health symptoms, social contagion is related to how symptoms may transmit across groups of people who may be more susceptible to influence by their peer group, and how these symptoms may be maintained through various interpersonal processes. Social and peer group influence has contributed to reinforcement of weight loss and/or excessive exercise in such a way that has contributed to risk for eating disorders among adolescent females, for example.[7] When applied to the experience of gender dysphoria, the social contagion theory reduces the complexity of gender dysphoria to nothing but peer group influences in ways that will likely be experienced as more antagonistic by people navigating gender identity questions.

subset of people within a broader, overarching shift in culture. I believe this shift is better accounted for by what Ian Hacking refers to as a "looping effect." Before I explain the looping effect, let me first discuss the splintering of gender categories.

Emerging Gender Identities

Some of these increases across generations could be a reflection of what I call "emerging gender identities."[8] Beyond transgender experiences in which a person experiences themselves as the opposite gender (a woman trapped inside the body of a man), we are seeing a rise in variations of nonnormative gender identity, with ever-expanding gender identity labels such as genderqueer, nonbinary, agender, bigender, androgyne, aporagender, graygender, demigender, demitrans, feminine-of-center, masculine-of-center, maverique, gender expansive, and gender creative, to name but a few. How did this splintering of gender categories come about?

Drawing on the work of Ian Hacking, I've suggested that there may be new ways people think about themselves in response to new categories, language, and terminology around gender. Let me give you one example. Mental health experts used to think of different experiences of gender as reflecting an identity problem. Since 2013, with the most recent revision of the *DSM*, mental health experts now no longer see different experiences of gender as an *identity* problem; rather, they see *distress* among those with different gender experiences as the problem. We moved from the *identity* being the problem, to the *distress* about the identity being the problem. That shift changed how a person (and the group of people who share similar experiences) thinks about themselves and even their history as a group. In response to these kinds of changes, people and people groups in some ways come into existence in response to how they are organized into categories and the meaning now given to those categorizations.

Mental health diagnoses are one way of categorizing people. Historically, there was a clear attempt in the transgender community to move away from medical and psychiatric language (e.g., *transsexual*) and toward language that people navigating atypical experiences of gender felt they could claim for themselves. That new language was *transgender*, which took individual and group experiences beyond mental health categories toward a more public identity. There are many steps involved in how these changes come about. Developments in mental health categorization and responses to medical and psychiatric terminology, in tandem with the growth of "experts" who determine what counts as true knowledge about gender, contribute to conjectural knowledge and taken-for-granted realities that end up on social media, in entertainment, and are otherwise reflected in society in compelling ways. This has been referred to as a "looping effect" that has been applied to a number of phenomena.[9]

If social contagion plays any role in people's diverse gender identities, it would be best to consider this phenomenon just one piece of an overarching looping pattern in society, where changes in language and categorization contribute to the further splintering of gender categories, the rise in the number of self-attributions associated with gender, and the renegotiation of individual and group characteristics.

The fact that a child has met transgender people online and then begins identifying as transgender doesn't invalidate the child's experience. But of course, prior to hearing from other transgender people, the child may not have had "transgender" as a category through which to interpret their experiences. The looping effect helps explain how people's awareness of a category shapes their interaction with that category, without social contagion necessarily being the culprit. When a child exploring gender identity uses the internet to connect with others who have similar experiences, that does not mean those online relationships *caused* the dysphoria. It may be that the child seeks out others to make sense of their own experience. We saw this with an emerging adult we met for a consultation who shared what online relationships meant to her:

> The internet became a fantastic thing. I learned a lot and connected to other people in [a] similar situation to me. I learned what was wrong with me and a way to fix it. However, I struggled with whether I wanted to transition because of both moral concerns and [my understanding] that people who do [transition] often have harder lives.

As I mentioned above, there is a difference between the *research* and the *interpretation* of research, a difference between

23

the *data* and what we *make* of the data. The looping effect is one way to try to make sense of the data of increasing trans identification. Others would see people with diverse gender identities as having always existed, apart from the existence of categories to describe them, and they interpret any increase in trans identification as an increase in societal awareness. Still others, as I mentioned, see these increases as something like a virus spread by way of social contagion, something that is "caught" through peer group interactions and influenced by trends toward transgender identities and community.

Another factor that may be at play in rising transgender identification is a broader cultural cynicism toward authority and norms. This cultural cynicism is in part the result of significant institutional failures, as we see with movements like #MeToo and #ChurchToo, as well as scandals and collapses at the highest levels of finance, banking, housing, education, and organized religion. It would make sense that some of this cynicism would be directed toward norms taught within organized religion, including norms surrounding sex and gender. This phenomenon is hard to point to directly, but it's likely part of the water we swim in. In other words, we are so immersed in this cynicism toward norms that we can forget it is a part of our lives at every turn.

People disagree about what is going on right now in the area of gender identity, gender dysphoria, and transgender experiences. Parents need to know that experts also currently disagree; we don't have the kind of consensus parents typically like to see when it comes to the care of their children. Professional organizations and experts in gender will claim consensus and claim to have true knowledge about gender, but keep in mind that even this apparent consensus is a predictable part of the looping effect I mentioned earlier. None of these claims are being handed down from on high with the kind of certainty you might want.

Bringing the Conversation Home

The question of how common transgender experiences and emerging gender identities are may come up in conversations between you and your child. An older child might ask if transgender identity was a conversation among your peers when you were a teen.

Child: Did your friends talk about being transgender when you were my age?

Parent: No, not really. It wasn't an experience that many people said they had, and it wasn't all that well known or understood. That doesn't mean we understand all of what's going on today, but it was talked about much less often when I was your age.

Child: So, it just didn't exist?

Parent: I wouldn't say that. There were well-known reports of people transitioning.

Child: What do you mean?

Parent: I'm thinking of when Chaz Bono, a celebrity, transitioned many years ago now. He is the child of very famous entertainers, Sonny and Cher. I can remember when Chaz transitioned because there just weren't as many instances of it. It also wasn't discussed in the same way as it is today.

Child: People are talking more about it today?

Parent: I think so, and it is on TV and the internet. It's become part of entertainment and a more mainstream conversation. You may or may not remember when Caitlyn Jenner transitioned in 2015. She had been Bruce Jenner prior to

25

her transition, and Bruce Jenner had been a
famous athlete who competed in the Olympics,
so her transition was definitely a big deal.

As a parent you could also be proactive and say to a child or
a teen, "It sounds like among the friends you have at school,
you know some people who are transgender. That wasn't an
experience that was as common when I was your age, but there
are more people today who talk about their experience of their
gender that way." Avoid any sense of putting your child or any
of their friends on trial. Stay curious, but don't let your curiosity lead to sharp questions that come across as accusations.

We are only getting at the question of prevalence here. This
is not the end of the conversation, but it marks the beginning
of a conversation that will be ongoing, one that we will return
to in each chapter of this book.

As we close this chapter, I want to help you as a parent take
a healthy posture toward this topic and the people represented
by it. Unfortunately, parents have few examples to turn to for
how to engage culturally explosive topics. We are mostly offered rather extreme options. I mentioned in the preface that
one extreme is that of the "culture warrior," or the person
whose greatest concern is to win a war against ideas they view
as threatening to Christianity. In my experience, parents who
take this route often do so out of fear—they fear the ways in
which society is changing and see the changes as a threat to their
children and their way of viewing the world. I am not saying
that there is nothing to be concerned about, but I do think as
parents we want to avoid fear-based ways of parenting, particularly if we take the posture of culture warrior in response to
those fears. Such a posture has to identify an enemy (after all,
you are at war), and that enemy often inadvertently becomes
the people navigating gender identity questions, which I don't
think reflects the heart of God toward them.

I also mentioned that the other extreme example for engagement is the "cultural capitulator." This is the person whose Christian worldview seems to have no bearing on the topics of sexuality and gender. They absorb every new idea and incorporate it into their way of seeing the world and never seem to critically evaluate it. As the broader culture begins to celebrate diverse gender identities, capitulators uncritically follow suit. But this will not position you as a parent to help your children explore the ideas behind the desire to celebrate. Nor will it encourage them to wrestle with how best to love people within the redemptive story of our shared faith.

Cultural Ambassador: Our Three Cs

As you and your child discuss cultural changes and real-life experiences of gender identity, I encourage you to think of yourself as a cultural ambassador. As a Christian, you are an ambassador of God's kingdom to the culture of which you are a part. You are engaging that culture in creative and practical ways. You are not at war with the culture, nor are you capitulating to the culture, as though everything the broader culture says about sex and gender is obviously correct. The posture of ambassadorship is what I call "convicted civility seasoned with compassion." These three Cs can guide the conversations you have with your kids about gender, gender identity, and their relationship to peers who identify as transgender or have transitioned.

Conviction. Convicted civility seasoned with compassion begins with convictions you hold as a Christian about sexuality and gender. What do you believe about sexuality and gender, and why? How is your "working knowledge" of sexuality and gender informed by your Christianity, your reading of the Bible, and other sources of information? It's essential to hold our convictions with humility, but it's also crucial to have a perspective based on Christian thought in this area so that you can parent your children well, helping them think critically about these topics. Perhaps reading this book will be a part of clarifying your convictions in your own mind.

Civility. When you think about convicted civility seasoned with compassion, think about how you are known to others in your spheres of influence—your home, obviously, but also your extended family, your neighborhood, your church, your place of employment, and so on. When polarizing topics come up, are you known as someone who can engage others without demonizing them? Can you treat people with the respect warranted them as people who bear the image of God? Can you sit with the tension that arises when positions on a topic are in conflict? It is increasingly apparent that the way we treat others in a diverse and pluralistic society is part of our Christian witness. Engaging others with civility sets a great example for your children.

Compassion. Finally, convicted civility seasoned with compassion means that you are known as being compassionate toward people navigating gender identity issues, including the language and categories used to describe experiences of gender today. In my experience, holding convictions and relating with civility can lead to compassion if we take some time to think about it. If we were talking about your child, would that influence how you would process what you are reading? Probably so. You could also picture this being the experience of your best friend's child—maybe that mental imagery will help you feel compassion toward people navigating these questions in their lives.

You can hold the conviction that there is a true north in these conversations—that there is a God whose plan for sexuality and gender is better than that offered by the broader culture—and at the same time appreciate that people who experience a discordant gender identity have to navigate a very challenging experience that they did not choose. In other words, it is possible to hold convictions about God's creational intent and also appreciate that some experiences of gender do not reflect that intent, nor are those experiences a choice. When you cease demonizing the "other side" and begin to relate to people with civility because of God's love for them, you allow room for compassion to grow in your heart. Compassion helps you show Christ to others, speaking into their confusion by pointing them to a good and loving Father whose love for them and plan for them is greater than anything else they have known.

We will return to these three Cs of relating and parenting on the topic of gender identity. But for now, begin to think about how these three Cs can be reflected in your life, and how you wish to be intentional about modeling each one for your children.

2

What causes someone to experience gender dysphoria?

We don't know.

The simple answer to this question—and the most accurate answer— is that we don't know.

Recent cultural shifts, especially the increasing prevalence of transgender identification, have added even greater uncertainty to the question of causation. To fully answer the question, we need to begin by discussing what *gender* is. Then we'll discuss gender dysphoria, and then some of the current thoughts on what causes gender dysphoria.

What Is Gender?

First let's distinguish between biological sex and gender. When *male* and *female* are used to refer to biological sex, we are referencing chromosomes (XX for females and XY for males), gonads (ovaries and testes), and genitalia (for females, these include the ovaries, uterus, and vagina; for males, these include the testes, penis, and scrotum).

When we talk about gender, we are generally referring to the cultural, psychological, and social aspects of male or female. Gender identity refers to a person's experience of themselves as a particular gender. For most people, this is a biological male's experience of himself as a boy or man, and a biological female's experience of herself as a girl or woman.

But there are exceptions to these categories. When we consider biological sex, we recognize that some people are born intersex; that is, they have an uncommon medical condition (sometimes referred to as a disorder of sex development) where they share reproductive tissue of both male and female, or may not be able to be readily identified as a boy or a girl at birth.

Likewise, when we consider gender identity, some people do not experience themselves as the gender that corresponds to their biological sex. A child who is biologically male may not experience himself as a boy; a biological female may not experience herself as a girl.

When a person's gender identity does not align with their biological sex and that misalignment is painful or distressing to them, we refer to that distress as *gender dysphoria*. If the distress is severe enough and the gender discordance is significant enough, they might warrant the diagnosis of Gender Dysphoria. Gender dysphoria resides along a continuum of severity or intensity; some people may not have a formal diagnosis but still experience some gender dysphoria. Gender dysphoria can vary in intensity from person to person; it can also ebb and flow in the same person over time, becoming a more or less intense experience.

When we ask, "What causes gender dysphoria?" we're often really asking, "What causes a person to experience a gender identity that does not reflect their biological sex?" I sometimes refer to this experience as *gender incongruence* or *gender discordance.* While a person who experiences gender incongruence might also experience gender dysphoria, not everyone who experiences incongruence would identify as having gender dysphoria.

It is important to recognize that many professionals in the field of gender identity are moving away from a focus on gender dysphoria and toward recognizing many diverse gender identities, where only a subset of those individuals experience gender dysphoria. When we focus as a profession on diverse gender identities, we do not tend to discuss what causes that diversity. Because of this shift, I suspect we will see fewer studies from the mental health community on the causes of diverse gender identities; such a framing would implicitly send the message that diverse gender identities are a concern, which they are not to the majority of gender specialists in mental health.

Transgender and Gender Dysphoria

You might be wondering about the relationship between gender dysphoria and transgender experiences. As I mentioned above, some people today view transgender experiences and emerging gender identities as not necessarily involving gender dysphoria. That is, they hold that any person can have any kind of gender identity, and only a subset of those people may experience gender dysphoria. This shift reflects a desire within the mental health community to get away from language that categorizes transgender people as having a disorder.

I can appreciate the desire to make this maneuver. The person experiencing a nonnormative gender identity finds this more validating. At the same time, Christians want to consider how gender is meant to relate to biological sex. Christians believe that when we were created, God intended our biological sex to line up with our gender identity, and when these don't align, something isn't functioning the way it was designed.

Gender dysphoria, for many Christians, means something has gone wrong—just as if our eyes or ears weren't seeing or hearing properly.

Even when gender dysphoria isn't severe enough to warrant a diagnosis, it can still be a part of people's experience of a discordant gender identity. There may come a time when the mainstream mental health community removes Gender Dysphoria from its official list of possible diagnoses. Transgender experiences and emerging gender identities would still exist, of course, but removing the experience of dysphoria from our diagnostic manual would reflect growing cultural affirmation of diverse gender identities. This shift would probably also inspire new ways of thinking about gender, which would in turn contribute to the looping effect I mentioned in chapter 1. This is what I think will occur in the next several years, so it might be worth considering how to prepare now. The sooner we reflect on how to engage these cultural messages, how to understand and critique them in light of Christian attitudes toward sexuality and gender, the better equipped we will be to respond to them as they arise.

Thoughts on Causes

When it comes to the causes of gender dysphoria, most psychologists and counselors who specialize in this field tend to gravitate to explanations that point to nature in the age-old nature vs. nurture debate. In other words, while we don't know what causes a person to experience gender dysphoria or identify with a gender that does not reflect their biological sex, specialists tend to assume that this experience or identity is the result of essentially biological processes that we do not fully understand at present.

In this discussion about causation, most of the research focuses on gender dysphoria, and may or may not involve self-identification as transgender. However, some research is focused on transgender experiences, which may or may not include dysphoria. I will focus in this section on gender dysphoria.

Part of the challenge in getting at what causes gender dysphoria is that there may be different pathways to the experience of gender dysphoria. For example, I mentioned above that a person could be born intersex. This is not the same as having gender dysphoria. However, a higher percentage of people who are intersex also report gender dysphoria, so there could be a pathway to gender dysphoria via intersex experiences.

In addition to intersex, the *DSM-5* distinguishes between early onset gender dysphoria and late-onset gender dysphoria. Early-onset dysphoria begins prior to puberty, whereas late-onset dysphoria begins at or after puberty. About 60 percent of transgender adults first experienced gender discordance prior to puberty, compared to 40 percent of transgender adults who first experienced gender discordance at the onset of puberty or after puberty.[1] Early-onset and late-onset experiences of dysphoria may not necessarily have different causes, but they do represent two different pathways into dysphoria. The two experiences seem to have long-term differences; for example, some research suggests that biological males with early-onset gender dysphoria tend to experience more persistent dysphoria, while males with late-onset dysphoria may experience more ebb and flow in their dysphoria.

What about other possible pathways into the experience of gender dysphoria? Some people have a sexual fetish related to cross-dressing activities. While this fetish itself is not gender dysphoria, gender dysphoria can develop over time in some cases, but this pathway to gender dysphoria is very different from the experiences of dysphoria reported by most people.

In recent years, we have also seen a remarkable increase in the number of adolescent biological females who report late-onset gender dysphoria. While there has been an increase in late-onset gender dysphoria among adolescent biological males as well, the sharpest increase has been among adolescent females. Some professionals speculate that this new trend in the data indicates yet another possible pathway to gender dysphoria.[2]

Of course, this overview of different pathways into dysphoria still doesn't tell us what *causes* gender dysphoria. Mental health professionals tend to identify the *onset* and the *course* of a condition rather than the *cause*. The onset is when a condition begins. In this case, onset has to do with the beginning signs of gender dysphoria. While the time of dysphoria's onset might rule out certain explanations of cause, it can't definitively prove any explanation of cause.

The course of a condition is the ebb and flow of the symptoms of that condition over time. The course has to do with the sequence of events associated with that condition in the life of the person. These events can give clues about causation, but they can't give answers. Like the onset of dysphoria, the course of gender dysphoria can vary significantly, and it still leaves the question of cause unanswered.

In short, we don't know what causes gender dysphoria. We do know that there seem to be multiple possible pathways to the same endpoint, a concept referred to as *equifinality*. There are probably multiple contributing factors that vary from person to person, and these factors may work differently depending on a person's pathway into dysphoria. This can be disappointing for parents to read. It is just where we are with the existing research. It is comparable to our lack of knowledge about what causes sexual orientation. However, in this case, much less research has been conducted on gender dysphoria than has been conducted on sexual orientation. There is still so much that we don't fully understand about the origins of discordant gender identities.

Bringing the Conversation Home

It's possible that the question of what causes gender dysphoria, transgender experiences, and emerging gender identities could come up in a conversation between you and your child. If it does, you could say something about the fact that we don't know what causes these experiences. Here is a sample exchange to provide you with some language:

Child: What causes people to be trans, anyway?

Parent: I was looking at that the other day, and what I found out is that researchers don't actually know what causes people to experience gender dysphoria or identity as transgender.

Child: Even the experts don't know?

Parent: That's what I'm reading. There is a lot of discussion about whether it is from nature or from nurture (or environment), but no one knows for sure.

Child: Okay, that's interesting. I was wondering about that.

Parent: One thing I did notice as I looked into all of this is that people don't choose one day to experience their gender identity in a way that doesn't match up with their biological sex. In other words, when people who identify as transgender say that they feel like their gender doesn't match their body, they don't choose to have that experience. It isn't just a matter of making a bad decision or a series of bad decisions. That's important to keep in mind. If you thought that they'd chosen to feel this way about their gender, you might just tell them to make better choices, and then everything would go away. That's not really that helpful. It sounds like most transgender people find themselves with an experience of gender that they didn't ask for, and they're trying to make sense of it.

Child: I figured that might be true. It would be strange to choose something like that.

Parent: Yeah, I think that's right. They probably face a bunch of choices moving forward in life, like how to respond to their experience of gender and how to cope with distress they may feel. Things like that. But what I'm reading is that they don't choose to have that disconnect itself, which kind of places them in a tough spot.

Child: I guess people I see don't seem to be in a tough spot. Like, with this one reality show, people just seem to be all about celebrating being trans.

Parent: I think what you are seeing is that there are many different experiences of being transgender. Some people find it to be a tough spot. They feel distress; they are weighing how best to respond to that distress. They aren't sure how it will be received in their community if they presented differently. But there are also those examples like you mentioned where people seem to be doing well. I wonder if both could be true.

Child: Sure, that makes sense. People have different ways of handling life experiences. I can see that.

Parent: People may also put their best foot forward if they are more public. That's kind of what you

see people do on social media. When you follow someone on social media, you may only
see the highlights of their day or week or year;
you may not see the things that are more challenging. Having said that, I'm sure there are
people who are doing well. It's just hard to say
for certain unless you really know someone
personally.

Some professionals make a distinction between gender dysphoria and transgender or other gender experiences. We will
likely see some additional research on what causes or contrib-
utes to gender dysphoria, and this will likely be considered
apart from celebrating multiple gender identities where the
cause is not studied as much—with the assumption that to
study a cause is to suggest that the experience warrants an
explanation. In other words, critics will say that the norm of
cisgender experience (when gender identity aligns with biological markers) doesn't have to account for itself, so neither should
variations in gender identity or experience.

Cultural Ambassador: Our Three Cs

Considering the three Cs of conviction, civility, and compassion, it's important to be able to speak to your child about certain convictions. You may find that what I am sharing from the
field of psychology and related fields informs your convictions,
and therefore informs your conversations with your children.
At the same time, as a Christian, you hold that the Bible is
authoritative and informs what you share with your children,
as we will discuss in greater detail in the next chapter.

In the case of theories of causation, since we really don't
know what causes gender dysphoria, and Scripture does not
appear to address it in any kind of detail, it is okay to say that

you don't know the answer to that. Speaking from a place of conviction doesn't mean that you need to give answers where neither science nor Scripture have given clear answers.

In my experience, exercising civility in conversations about what causes people to be transgender or experience gender dysphoria has to do with agreeing to disagree when someone is adamant that they know why a person is transgender (for example, they "fell away from God") or why they themselves are transgender (for example, "I was born this way"). I don't think experiences of nonnormative gender identity are the result of disobedience to God, nor do I think we know enough today to conclude that a person was born transgender. We can respectfully hear a person out and listen to why they believe as they do, but we can also agree to disagree. It's okay to hear someone else's explanation of causation and then respond, "Thanks for sharing that. I feel like I just don't know at the moment."

When it comes to compassion in these conversations about the causes of discordant gender identity, we can cultivate a deeper empathy for people who experience gender dysphoria. Recall that dysphoria is the opposite of euphoria. Euphoria is a positive emotion—it is high and thrilling. Dysphoria is a negative emotion—it is low and discouraging. As people try to manage their dysphoria through creative means, they may not discuss it in terms of alleviating pain, but that is much of what they are doing. They may frame their experience as their new self, their true identity, or something along those lines. That makes sense too. You don't have to agree with everything a person asserts about their experience, but keep in mind that a sense of self often comes in response to what has been discordant and painful at times. We can be compassionate about this pain and about what it may be like to not know the cause behind the pain.

3

What does the Bible say about being transgender?

Not much.

Again, as we did in the last chapter in discussing possible causes of different gender identities, let me provide a little more context to this answer.

The Bible doesn't really say a lot about gender dysphoria, transgender experiences, or emerging gender identities. At least, it doesn't say much about these terms directly. That doesn't mean the Bible doesn't speak into this conversation, but we have to be careful not to try to get the Bible to say things it either doesn't say or wasn't intending to say.

This comes back to how we approach the Bible and our assumptions about its scope in addressing different phenomena in the world—especially modern phenomena that weren't occurring in the same way when the Bible was written. I recommend taking some time to reflect on what you believe the purpose of the Bible is and how it informs us about different topics. Let me share a few of my thoughts.

I view the Bible as without error when addressing the topics it is meant to address. The Bible is sometimes thought of as a letter from God meant to express his love for us. It is a collection of books that primarily testify to how God chose to reveal himself to us through a particular group of people—the ancient Israelites—and ultimately, through his son, Jesus, through whom we may experience redemption and the forgiveness of sins.

When I say the Bible is without error when addressing the topics it is meant to address, I recognize that there are some topics the Bible does not intend to address. It is not a science book, for example. I don't turn to it for a scientific explanation of the universe. Such an approach would lead to a misreading—categorizing the mustard seed as the "smallest of all seeds" (Matthew 13:31–32), for example. I don't expect the Bible to account for chemical reactions or aid in the measurement of the speed of light. It is not a medical textbook. I don't turn to it for instructions on how to remove a person's gall bladder. It will not provide my dentist with the information needed to fill a cavity. The Bible is also not a psychiatric handbook. I don't turn to it to understand and treat eating disorders, just as I wouldn't turn to it for the conceptualization and treatment of gender dysphoria.

Chapter and Verse vs. Principles

Although the Bible does not say much about transgender experiences, I don't want to suggest that it is irrelevant to the conversation. That's not what I am saying at all.

In sharing the story of redemption with us, the Bible reveals important information about sexuality and gender. But it doesn't function as a handbook on sexuality and gender, nor is it a protocol for counseling people who have discordant experiences of gender identity.

So how do we gain insight from the Bible on this topic?

One approach is "chapter and verse"; the other approach is using principles derived from broad themes.

A friend called me recently to ask about transgender experiences. The topic had come up at work; he had a coworker who was exploring Christianity and wanted to know what the Bible says about transgender experiences. My friend was asking for a chapter and verse.

I could understand this impulse; I have the same impulse. Many Christians are chapter-and-verse Christians; that is, they want a quick answer from a specific chapter and verse from the Bible that will settle the matter. Murder is wrong. We have a chapter and verse for that. Stealing is wrong. We have a chapter and verse for that. And, indeed, some topics lend themselves to this approach, although most topics require a little more thoughtful engagement to apply the chapter and verse to the present moment. But the topics of gender dysphoria and transgender experiences are not "chapter and verse" kinds of topics.

Deuteronomy 22:5 prohibits cross-dressing behavior. It reads, "A woman must not wear men's clothing, nor a man wear women's clothing, for the LORD your God detests anyone who does this." But how do we apply this verse today? Six verses later, Deuteronomy 22:11 prohibits wearing blends of wool and linen, but we understand this prohibition in light of its cultural background. Scholars suggest that such a blend was banned because of a connection to some Egyptian idolatrous or immoral practice.[1] Since this connection no longer exists today, the prohibition no longer applies. As a result of scholarship on interpretation and application, few people object to wool-linen blends in their clothes.

So what about Deuteronomy 22:5? One interpretation of the prohibition on cross-dressing is that the Canaanites engaged in ritual practices that incorporated cross-sex dress and sexual behavior.[2] Since these ritual practices (if they used to exist) no longer exist today, how might that change our application of the prohibition today? What if there are fewer clear distinctions between "men's clothes" and "women's clothes" in a society where more androgynous attire is available? Also, does a person's motivation for cross-dressing matter? The people I've known who preferred clothing associated with the other gender often had a wide range of reasons for their preference. I have met with people who wore such clothing to manage their dysphoria, to express a sense of self, to push back against social norms, as a fetish associated with sexual arousal, in response to anxiety, out of boredom, and many other motivations. The term *cross-dress* would also need to be defined a little more clearly. Clothing styles vary from culture to culture. In our culture, some clothing is more or less gendered, while some styles are more androgynous or overlap considerably. In any case, I would be particularly concerned to see the church tighten the ratchets on variations in hairstyle or clothing that are widely accepted in the broader church culture but disallowed for those who are seeking some relief from their gender dysphoria. (If, for example, most women are welcome to have short hair, short hair should also be welcome for women who find that longer and more "feminine" hairstyles make their dysphoria worse.)

It makes sense, then, to avoid cut-and-paste approaches or chapter-and-verse approaches to passages like Deuteronomy 22:5 by attempting to apply them directly to the experience of gender dysphoria. If the chapter-and-verse approach isn't helpful, what is the alternative?

The alternative is to look at principles derived from the broad themes in Scripture related to the topics of sexuality and gender. In other words, when the Bible does speak to matters of sexuality and gender, we can try to get a better idea for the context of those discussions and for what God may be trying to say to the people who were originally being spoken to. With discernment, we can consider how God may want us to apply a passage of

Scripture today, even when that passage was not explicitly written to address all the questions we hold about a topic.[3]

Themes from Creation Stories

When we look at the stories of creation in Genesis 1 and 2, we read about the creation of all that is, including and culminating with the creation of people. The people we learn about are sexed male and female.

Here is the account from Genesis 1:26–31:

> Then God said, "Let us make mankind in our image, in our likeness, so that they may rule over the fish in the sea and the birds in the sky, over the livestock and all the wild animals, and over all the creatures that move along the ground."
>
> So God created mankind in his own image,
>   in the image of God he created them;
>   male and female he created them.
>
> God blessed them and said to them, "Be fruitful and increase in number; fill the earth and subdue it. Rule over the fish in the sea and the birds in the sky and over every living creature that moves on the ground."
>
> Then God said, "I give you every seed-bearing plant on the face of the whole earth and every tree that has fruit with seed in it. They will be yours for food. And to all the beasts of the earth and all the birds in the sky and all the creatures that move along the ground—everything that has the breath of life in it—I give every green plant for food." And it was so.
>
> God saw all that he had made, and it was very good. And there was evening, and there was morning—the sixth day.

There are many directions you can go with this account of creation, but the main point we are considering is whether and how Scripture speaks into sexuality and gender. What can we say from this first account?

The major themes we see addressed are the creation of humankind in God's image; the charge to exercise responsible dominion over the rest of creation; the distinction by sex (male and female); and the charge toward increasing in number (procreation), which speaks to the biologically complementary relationship between the two sexes. The goodness of all that has been created is also a part of this discussion.

We also see in this first creation account a distinction made between men and women. God did not have to create two sexes, but he chose to create two sexes. We can explore the question of why God chose to do that, and we can debate whether the creation story accounts for all possible experiences of sexuality and gender, but this account definitely distinguishes male and female in ways that inform other practical considerations. This distinction is tied to the charge to increase (the charge toward procreation). The goodness of creation and the creation of two sexes suggests some good and beautiful predisposition of being that contains something of God's creativity in humanness.

Other practical applications of the male/female distinction have to do with the meaning of marriage and the question of divorce. For example, in one instance when Jesus was being provoked by the religious leaders of his day, their conversation turned to divorce. Jesus had responded to those leaders by referencing the creation story in Genesis 1.

Matthew records this exchange in chapter 19:

> When Jesus had finished saying these things, he left Galilee and went into the region of Judea to the other side of the Jordan. Large crowds followed him, and he healed them there.
>
> Some Pharisees came to him to test him. They asked, "Is it lawful for a man to divorce his wife for any and every reason?"
>
> "Haven't you read," he replied, "that at the beginning the Creator 'made them male and female,' and said, 'For this reason

a man will leave his father and mother and be united to his wife, and the two will become one flesh'? So they are no longer two, but one flesh. Therefore what God has joined together, let no one separate."

vv. 1–6

Notice that Jesus referenced the creation story in his response to the Pharisees. He seemed to assume there were established norms from creation that he could point to in order to help the teachers of the law understand underlying principles related to God's purposes for marriage. So too we can consider what we can derive from the norms of creation to inform our understanding of sex and gender.

Let's turn now to the second account of creation in Genesis 2:7–25:

Then the LORD God formed a man from the dust of the ground and breathed into his nostrils the breath of life, and the man became a living being.

Now the LORD God had planted a garden in the east, in Eden; and there he put the man he had formed. The LORD God made all kinds of trees grow out of the ground—trees that were pleasing to the eye and good for food. In the middle of the garden were the tree of life and the tree of the knowledge of good and evil.

A river watering the garden flowed from Eden; from there it was separated into four headwaters. The name of the first is the Pishon; it winds through the entire land of Havilah, where there is gold. (The gold of that land is good; aromatic resin and onyx are also there.) The name of the second river is the Gihon; it winds through the entire land of Cush. The name of the third river is the Tigris; it runs along the east side of Ashur. And the fourth river is the Euphrates.

The LORD God took the man and put him in the Garden of Eden to work it and take care of it. And the LORD God commanded the man, "You are free to eat from any tree in the garden; but you must not eat from the tree of the knowledge of good and evil, for when you eat from it you will certainly die."

The LORD God said, "It is not good for the man to be alone. I will make a helper suitable for him."

Now the LORD God had formed out of the ground all the wild animals and all the birds in the sky. He brought them to the man to see what he would name them; and whatever the man called each living creature, that was its name. So the man gave names to all the livestock, the birds in the sky and all the wild animals.

But for Adam no suitable helper was found. So the LORD God caused the man to fall into a deep sleep; and while he was sleeping, he took one of the man's ribs and then closed up the place with flesh. Then the LORD God made a woman from the rib he had taken out of the man, and he brought her to the man.

The man said,

"This is now bone of my bones
    and flesh of my flesh;
  she shall be called 'woman,'
    for she was taken out of man."

That is why a man leaves his father and mother and is united to his wife, and they become one flesh.

Adam and his wife were both naked, and they felt no shame.

As with the first account of creation, there are many directions you can go with this second account. Recall that our main emphasis is to consider whether and how Scripture speaks into sexuality and gender. What can we say from this second account? We see more emphasis placed on the relationship between the man and the woman—that is, how they are made of the same substance, and how they are of the same kind as compared to the other creatures Adam would name. There is something of their sameness and of how they reflect a complementary relationship with one another that is unique in comparison to the rest of creation.

Taken together, the stories of creation contain important, informative principles about the male and female sexes that many Christians throughout history say lay the foundation for marriage. This marriage relationship is instructive for the church because God uses the analogy of bride and bridegroom to depict the church being prepared for the return of Jesus. God uses the same analogy to describe his relationship to Israel in the Old Testament. This analogy reflects God's commitment to his people, even when his people, the Israelites, were unfaithful to him, even when they prostituted themselves to other nations through their idolatry.

The Fall Affects Our Sexuality and Gender

Our sexuality and gender, and our experiences of ourselves as sexual and gendered beings, are affected by the fall. But sexuality and gender aren't the only parts of ourselves this is true of. All of creation is affected by the fall.

The story of the fall is recorded in Genesis 3:1–24.

Now the serpent was more crafty than any of the wild animals the LORD God had made. He said to the woman, "Did God really say, 'You must not eat from any tree in the garden'?"

The woman said to the serpent, "We may eat fruit from the trees in the garden, but God did say, 'You must not eat fruit from the tree that is in the middle of the garden, and you must not touch it, or you will die.'"

"You will not certainly die," the serpent said to the woman. "For God knows that when you eat from it your eyes will be opened, and you will be like God, knowing good and evil."

When the woman saw that the fruit of the tree was good for food and pleasing to the eye, and also desirable for gaining wisdom, she took some and ate it. She also gave some to her husband, who was with her, and he ate it. Then the eyes of both of them were opened, and they realized they were naked; so they sewed fig leaves together and made coverings for themselves.

Then the man and his wife heard the sound of the LORD God as he was walking in the garden in the cool of the day, and they hid from the LORD God among the trees of the garden. But the LORD God called to the man, "Where are you?"

He answered, "I heard you in the garden, and I was afraid because I was naked; so I hid."

And he said, "Who told you that you were naked? Have you eaten from the tree that I commanded you not to eat from?"

The man said, "The woman you put here with me—she gave me some fruit from the tree, and I ate it."

Then the LORD God said to the woman, "What is this you have done?"

The woman said, "The serpent deceived me, and I ate."

So the LORD God said to the serpent, "Because you have done this,

> "Cursed are you above all livestock
>> and all wild animals!
>> You will crawl on your belly
>> and you will eat dust
>> all the days of your life.
>> And I will put enmity
>> between you and the woman,
>> and between your offspring and hers;
>> he will crush your head,
>> and you will strike his heel."

To the woman he said,

> "I will make your pains in childbearing very severe;
>> with painful labor you will give birth to children.
>> Your desire will be for your husband,
>> and he will rule over you."

To Adam he said, "Because you listened to your wife and ate fruit from the tree about which I commanded you, 'You must not eat from it,'

> "Cursed is the ground because of you;
>   through painful toil you will eat food from it
>   all the days of your life.
> It will produce thorns and thistles for you,
>   and you will eat the plants of the field.
> By the sweat of your brow
>   you will eat your food
> until you return to the ground,
>   since from it you were taken;
> for dust you are
>   and to dust you will return."

Adam named his wife Eve, because she would become the mother of all the living.

The Lord God made garments of skin for Adam and his wife and clothed them. And the Lord God said, "The man has now become like one of us, knowing good and evil. He must not be allowed to reach out his hand and take also from the tree of life and eat, and live forever." So the Lord God banished him from the Garden of Eden to work the ground from which he had been taken. After he drove the man out, he placed on the east side of the Garden of Eden cherubim and a flaming sword flashing back and forth to guard the way to the tree of life.

Again, there is much to the account of the fall that we could get into, but we are focusing on sexuality and gender and whether there are lessons in Scripture to inform our understanding of gender identity today.

The effect of the fall on sexuality and gender is broad and considerable. Scripture speaks to the strain between males and females. I have suggested elsewhere that the fall introduced the possibility of objectifying others in ways that were not present prior to the fall.[4] Perhaps the most widespread example of this objectification is the contemporary pornography industry. But even looking at another human being with lust is an expression of the same principle of fallenness: We are now able to view others as objects for our own gratification. People can be valued for how they benefit someone else's sexual appetite rather than valued for their intrinsic worth as made in God's image.

Because of the fall, people can experience shame in their sexuality. The experience of shame was not possible at creation and before the fall. Regardless of whether shame is *inevitable* after the fall or whether it is simply an experience that became *possible* because of the fall, shame does appear to be widespread in contemporary culture. It can frequently be tied to experiences that impinge on our personhood, including sexual trauma and related experiences.

The fall makes it possible to foster environments that express and reinforce toxic masculinity, which is pervasive in Christian circles. We can also send unhelpful messages about femininity that are more cultural than biblical. If we discuss gender dysphoria as a result of a fallen creation, we have to first speak to how the fall touches so much of our experience of sexuality and gender among those who are cisgender.

The account of the fall provides us with important informative principles about the state of creation, including human existence, our sexuality and gender, and limitations and challenges that are present in different people's experiences and to differing degrees on this side of eternity.

Themes from the Time "Between the Times"

The Christian holds that we are not abandoned to our fallen state. Christ's redemptive act on the cross realized a redemption of all of creation that has been described as the time "between the times" by Oscar Cullmann. Cullmann likened this time in redemptive history to the time in World War II between D-Day and V-E Day, when the allies knew that they would win the war but still had to fight some of their fiercest battles:

> *The decisive battle in a war may already have occurred in a relatively early stage of the war, and yet the war still continues.* Although the decisive effect of that battle is perhaps not recognized by all, it nevertheless already means victory. But the war must still be carried on for an undefined time, until "Victory Day." Precisely this is the situation of which the New Testament is conscious, as a result of the recognition of the new division of time; the revelation consists precisely in the fact of the proclamation that *that event on the cross, together with the resurrection which followed, was the already concluded decisive battle.*[5]

The time "between the times" is *now*—that is, after the resurrection and before the consummation. It should not be lost on us that consummation is also a reference to completing or fulfilling a marriage commitment through the act of sexual intimacy. This is the consummation of the relationship between the bridegroom, who is Jesus, and the bride, that is, the church.

When we look for themes of redemption in Scripture, we can draw upon theological truths from passages such as Romans 8:19–22:[6]

> For the creation waits in eager expectation for the children of God to be revealed. For the creation was subjected to frustration, not by its own choice, but by the will of the one who subjected it, in hope that the creation itself will be liberated from its bondage to decay and brought into the freedom and glory of the children of God.
>
> We know that the whole creation has been groaning as in the pains of childbirth right up to the present time.

Creation is anticipating its own liberation from sin and decay. There are two kinds of anticipation. One is the excitement of an unveiling. I recall my children's anticipation on Christmas morning, coming downstairs at the break of day (or earlier!) to see what gifts might have their names on them. It was an existential moment of possibility filled with the eager anticipation of blessing.

The other kind of anticipation—the one mentioned in Romans 8:19–22—is the anticipation in the experience of pain, such as a woman ready to give birth, an eagerness to replace pangs of childbirth with the celebration of new life. It is moving through something painful and difficult to get to a promised destination. This is the kind of anticipation we are seeing in all of creation as it awaits its future.

When we think of the many painful conditions people face, including both health conditions and mental health conditions, we often recognize that something is not functioning properly.[7] For example, since fourth grade I have experienced a condition called vitiligo. Vitiligo is a skin condition that causes the loss of skin pigmentation. It occurs when the cells that produce pigment stop functioning properly. While there are some treatments available for vitiligo, it is a condition that cannot be cured. It is a nonmoral reality that exists in a fallen world rather than a reflection of personal sin, even though that is very much the way such a condition has been viewed previously. I can't imagine myself without vitiligo, nor can I imagine who I would be had my life and relationships not been shaped by my experience of this condition. Vitiligo exists "between the times," and people with skin conditions like vitiligo are awaiting their own redemption, an eager anticipation of proper functioning.

Or consider a condition like hearing loss. Hearing loss, like vision impairment or vision loss, was at one time thought to be the result of sinful choices a person made, or choices made by a person's parents (John 9:1–3). But that is not how we view hearing loss today. Now we recognize that there is something not functioning properly.[8] As a result of these insights, a concern like hearing loss is viewed as a nonmoral reality. Hearing loss exists "between the times," as if the ears of those with hearing loss are awaiting their own redemption, an eager anticipation of proper functioning.

Likewise, gender dysphoria is properly thought of as existing in the world as a consequence of the fall (though not simply the consequence of individual sinful choices). But something is not functioning as it was intended. Just as with vitiligo or hearing loss, accounts of gender dysphoria should pull compassion forward. Gender dysphoria is a more ethically complex topic, however, and it brings with it layers of messaging about sex and gender, cultural expectations, norms, corresponding behaviors for management, and so on.

Responding Redemptively to Fallen Realities

This brings us to how we deal redemptively with fallen realities. We can see the compassion Jesus demonstrated to people with various conditions or experiences, some of which were thought to be the result of personal or parental sin at that time. These included those who were sick or had a range of diseases (Luke 4:40), blindness (John 9:1–3), muteness (Matthew 9:32), and other concerns (Luke 6:19).

As we consider additional circumstances that did involve morally impermissible behavior, we can also look at how Jesus responded to people on matters of sexuality and gender. Perhaps the most well-known exchange is the story of the woman caught in adultery, as recorded in John 8:1–11:

> But Jesus went to the Mount of Olives.
> At dawn he appeared again in the temple courts, where all the people gathered around him, and he sat down to teach

them. The teachers of the law and the Pharisees brought in a woman caught in adultery. They made her stand before the group and said to Jesus, "Teacher, this woman was caught in the act of adultery. In the Law Moses commanded us to stone such women. Now what do you say?" They were using this question as a trap, in order to have a basis for accusing him.

But Jesus bent down and started to write on the ground with his finger. When they kept on questioning him, he straightened up and said to them, "Let any one of you who is without sin be the first to throw a stone at her." Again he stooped down and wrote on the ground.

At this, those who heard began to go away one at a time, the older ones first, until only Jesus was left, with the woman still standing there. Jesus straightened up and asked her, "Woman, where are they? Has no one condemned you?"

"No one, sir," she said.

"Then neither do I condemn you," Jesus declared. "Go now and leave your life of sin."

In this remarkably complex situation, Jesus is once again being set up by those who hold religious authority around him to see what he will do in various situations. While they are testing Jesus's position on adultery, the scenario they've created involves an actual encounter with a woman whose life could very well have been forfeited. Jesus's response is multifaceted. He challenges the religious leaders' assumptions of what needs to happen next. He knows their hearts, and his response tells them he knows their hearts. They face the decision of whether to move forward with punishment of the woman or to move toward more scrutiny of their own motives. Jesus also demonstrates compassion to the woman, both in relation to her sin and in relation to the way the Pharisees have used her to test Jesus. She is a chess piece in a larger contest that she knows nothing about. In the midst of his compassion, Jesus also holds convictions about sexual fidelity, and his final words to the woman are to direct her toward that end ("go and sin no more").

There is a nuance here that Christians today ought to emulate. Our exchanges should be a mixture of convictions, civility, and compassion, and we should pray for wisdom, discernment, and prudence in how we carry and embody this mixture in our exchanges with others and in what we model for our children. Our responses should reflect insight into redemptive purposes in the encounters we have with others. In this passage, Jesus's redemptive purpose for the religious leaders was to direct them away from a position of testing Jesus toward a position of humility and self-scrutiny. For the woman caught in sin, Jesus's redemptive purpose was for her to see her value to God the Father as experienced in this moment with Jesus the Son. She was of worth to God. Her present circumstances did not reflect her value as a child of the king. It might well be that gratitude for God's mercy and love ultimately led her to repentance.

The arc of redemption bends toward the consummation of all things. People will sometimes ask whether a person will be transgender or experience gender dysphoria in eternity. I suppose we could ask a similar question about my experience of vitiligo or someone else's hearing loss. My own view is that I don't think these conditions as we experience them today extend into the consummation of all things, but who we have become in our experience of them does extend into eternity, if that makes sense. It would be hard to separate who we are from how we have carried enduring realities throughout our lives. So, for example, I will no longer experience vitiligo in eternity, but I will continue to be a person whose life story has been shaped in some ways by that experience. In the same way, a person who experiences dysphoria could find relief from that dysphoria in eternity without losing the wisdom and maturity they gained through their experience in this lifetime.

But I am only speculating. Scripture doesn't provide us with many details about consummation or glorification. The primary focus of what is shared with us has to do with the eternal reign of Jesus. Eternity won't be so much about us, but about him. Who we are will be perfectly aligned with God's purposes as we praise him and enter into a more full and complete relationship with him.

There are important, informative principles about redemption and glorification that we can derive from Scripture and apply to the topics of sexuality and gender. We are in a time of "now and not yet" when we have a foretaste of the redemption and consummation of creation but do not fully experience it. We are moving toward alignment with God's purposes, which are only glimpsed to differing degrees in the present moment.

When we read the full scope of Scripture through these distinct acts, we see that God's creational intent reflected male/female distinctions. There is an assumed, corresponding relationship between what we today think of as gender identity—a person's experience of themselves as a man or woman (or a boy or girl)—and what we today think of as biological markers—their chromosomes, gonads, and genitalia. This isn't taught explicitly, nor would we expect it to be taught explicitly, since Scripture is not a medical or psychological handbook. But what is presented are norms and function from creation in terms of gender identity corresponding to one's embodied self.

The effects of the fall are wide-reaching, touching all of creation. Our sexuality and gender are not immune to those effects. Much of how the fall touches creation has little to do with gender dysphoria; it shows up in our many struggles with reducing people to objects, mistreatment of others, a desire for relationships outside of the context God intended, and so on. But a discordant gender identity (one that does not align with biological markers) and the corresponding distress we refer to as gender dysphoria do not appear to be what God intended for human flourishing.

There is creational intent, and then there are departures from that creation that are not the result of choice, not willful disobedience, but simply variations that occur in a fallen world, nonmoral realities that we should respond to with grace and compassion. We should not exclaim that a person has sinned in how they experience themselves, nor should we celebrate that experience as a reflection of God's creativity.

Let me close this section by returning to a couple of observations I made earlier. First, we should be clear that some or even most cisgender experiences also depart from the created order of our behavior and self-understanding as men and women. Toxic masculinity, as noted above, is pervasive in Christendom and by no means part of creational intent, cisgender though it may be. Transgender and nonbinary experiences of gender may not reflect what God originally intended. However, in all cases, we should help people grow in the ways the Bible says we should grow: closer to Jesus and more in his likeness through the work of the Holy Spirit.

Second, is it possible that there is some quality or predisposition of being that, in its fallen form, reflects dysphoria, yet still is good and beautiful and contains something of God's creativity in it, in the humanness that accompanies dysphoria? If God created male and female in order to, as Heather Looy once put it, reflect the "genderfulness of God,"[9] then perhaps it is possible that people who suffer from gender dysphoria might be a reflection of God's creativity in this sense (in this aspect, this predisposition of being), even if the discordance and corresponding dysphoria as such is a mark of fallenness.

The answers to these questions are beyond the scope of this chapter, but I want to at least help you as parents begin to think through the complexity of the topic. It is especially important to think through complexity when we discuss a Christian view of a topic, particularly a topic with limited direct biblical reference points. Much of what I have discussed in this chapter is what I will refer to as a conservative or traditional or historical Christian perspective, just to recognize that thoughtful Christians are grappling with these topics, and some have reached different conclusions about how to best understand them.

Bringing the Conversation Home

Whenever we speak about "what God thinks" about something—anything—we should do so with humility, because we may not get it perfectly right. Not getting something perfectly right can quickly take us down the path of getting something wrong. But at the same time, as parents, we are charged with raising and educating our children in the Christian faith, including how the Christian faith informs our understanding of important aspects of human experience, such as our sexuality and gender.

It is encouraging to me that we, as parents, are not raising and educating our children in isolation. We raise them in a household that is connected to a local church that is connected to a branch of Christianity that is connected to and rooted in historic Christian thought on these topics.

Indeed, it is when we depart from historic Christianity that we should especially give pause to our teaching and instruction, as we have warnings from Scripture about new trends in thinking that are not a reflection of the teachings handed down to us. Of course, we also scrutinize traditions and confirm that current teaching is a reflection of God's heart toward a topic and the people represented by that topic.

There will likely be many opportunities to discuss what the Bible says about a topic, and I do encourage parents to think about the four acts of the biblical drama—creation, the fall, redemption, and consummation—to remind their child and themselves where we are in the story, what it means to experience redemption, and what it means to move toward the consummation of all things. You might not reference these four acts in a conversation with your child, but you can have them as an anchor nonetheless.

Child: I wonder what God thinks of the transgender stuff.

Parent: That's a great question! What do you think?

Child: I don't know. I mean, I've been taught God created boys and girls, so I'm not sure what he'd say about people being transgender, you know?

Parent: Yeah, I think a lot of people are trying to make sense of it, but I like that you remembered that God says something important about boys and girls at creation. He made us as male or female. He said that this was good.

Child: I guess it's confusing that people say things like, "God doesn't make mistakes." I've heard people say that when they say mean things about transgender people, and I've also heard transgender people online say it to celebrate who they are.

Parent: That sounds like one of those sayings that has become kind of a weapon people use against one another. What do you think people mean when they say it?

Child: I'm not sure. I think those who disagree with transgender people seem to be saying that God didn't make you that way, because he doesn't make mistakes, so if you are that way, you are a mistake, like, it's not a good choice you've made. But trans people seem to say it to say that God did make them this way and that they are not a mistake.

Parent: We were saying a minute ago that being a boy or a girl is a good of creation. But we also know that while creation is good, creation has been affected by the fall. All of creation experienced the fall when our first parents disobeyed God, so there were consequences to that. Things are not the way they were originally intended. That could also be true of our experience of our sexuality or gender—all of us, not just people who experience their gender this way.

Child: That makes sense. Maybe not everything is exactly the way it was supposed to be.

Parent: That could help explain some differences that people experience. But God comes alongside us and is present with us in our circumstances. He promises to always be with us and to guide us if we trust in him.

Child: I'm glad for that.

Parent: If a friend of yours was experiencing gender identity questions, that friend could also know that God loves him and will be with him and will walk this out with him through his life. He won't be alone.

Child: That's encouraging to know.

Cultural Ambassador: Our Three Cs

As we conclude this chapter on what the Bible says about gender and gender identity, we want to think about ambassadorship and our three Cs of conviction, civility, and compassion. Scripture does speak to sexuality and gender, although as we have seen, Scripture does not go into great detail, nor does it specifically address what we refer to as gender dysphoria.

Many of the passages of Scripture that address sexuality and gender do so in specific instances of, say, the apostle Paul addressing a concern in a church. But we do see that sexuality and gender are addressed at different places throughout the scope of Scripture and can be understood with reference to creation, the fall, redemption, and consummation. Much of what is reflected in Scripture appears to be taken-for-granted expectations for what we today refer to as biological sex, gender, and gender identity. We can and should hold convictions about God's creational intent, but also about the reality of the fall and the ways in which the fall may affect our sexuality and experience of gender. We can also consider what we believe to be true about redemption, about how God may be at work in a person's life as they know him better.

Civility in conversations about the Bible can show up in several ways. We can demonstrate civility when talking to people who do not view the Bible as a source of authority in their own lives and see no reason to turn to it on matters of sexuality and gender. We can also be civil in our conversations with those who do seek the Bible as a source of authority but who disagree with us on any claims of a true north in what we believe Scripture teaches about sexuality and gender. This can be in terms of creational intent, the effects of the fall, and questions about redemption and moving toward consummation.

I believe compassion is needed the most when we engage with people directly affected by this topic. That includes the person navigating gender identity and their family. The person who is experiencing a discordant gender identity and who is a Christian is likely going to be asking a lot of questions about God, about God's will, about their own experience of suffering, and about what God wants for them moving forward. We can show compassion to that person even and especially if we are invited to join them in discerning what the Bible says about these experiences.

PART 2

Talking with Your Kids

4

What do I tell my child about gender in general?

Gender reveal parties are all the rage today. Some young couples set up a gender reveal piñata that will burst with either pink or blue confetti, while others swing a baseball bat at a powder-filled baseball to reveal the gender of their child. Fans of the Harry Potter books have delighted in the use of the sorting hat, while *Star Wars* fans have revealed the gender by colorful light sabers. Gender reveals featuring dragon eggs and Pokémon balls have also tapped into iconic cultural memes that have captured our imaginations. There seems to be no shortage of creative ways to share with family and friends the wonderful news—whether a couple is having a boy or a girl.

These lighthearted events suggest that the vast majority of people in our society subscribe to the view that gender and sex are tied together in normative ways. As we have seen, this is the Christian view as well. While we teach and celebrate these norms, we also know that there are exceptions to the norms, and that these exceptions are to be expected. We are to love and celebrate personhood in these instances as well.

Discordant Gender Identity

Gender reveal parties, then, are also teachable moments when parents talk about gender with their own children. What you say to your child about gender will vary somewhat depending on their age and where you are in discussing related concepts like sexuality.

A child typically develops the awareness that they are a boy or a girl between the ages of two and four. That is the time when a child understands what the words *boy* and *girl* mean, and how those words apply to themselves and to others. Of course, parents have already been talking to their child in gendered language prior to this self-awareness: "Aren't you just a handsome boy!" "Aren't you such a wonderful boy!" or "Aren't you a beautiful girl!" "You are so smart, little lady." There are countless ways in which parents communicate something about gender very early on as they talk with their child.

Recall that gender generally refers to the cultural and social aspects of being male or female. When we talk about male and female, we are usually referencing biological sex in terms of chromosomes (XX for females and XY for males), gonads (ovaries and testes), and genitalia (for females, these include the ovaries, uterus, and vagina; for males, these include the testes, penis, and scrotum).

Gender, then, refers to the cultural and social aspects of being male or female, including how masculine or feminine a person experiences themselves to be, usually with reference to social and cultural expectations. Both masculinity and femininity as concepts are tied to biological sex, but any discussion of masculinity and femininity will be anchored more in social and cultural aspects of being a man or a woman.

Gender identity refers to a person's experience of themselves as a particular gender. For most people, this is a biological male's experience of himself as a boy or man, and a biological female's experience of herself as a girl or woman.

But there are exceptions to these categories, of course. When we consider biological sex, we recognize that some people are born intersex—that is, they have a medical condition where they share reproductive tissue of male and female or may not be able to be readily identified as a boy or a girl at birth. The most common intersex conditions[1] include:

- Klinefelter's syndrome (1 in 1,000 births)
- Congenital adrenal hyperplasia (1 in 13,000 births)
- Testosterone biosynthetic defects (1 in 13,000 births)
- Androgen insensitivity syndrome (1 in 13,000 births)
- Gonadal dysgenesis (1 in 150,000 births)

The reason I point to a few of the many medical conditions that can be reflected among those who are intersex is to say that Christians can recognize and teach a sex binary as creational intent while also recognizing that there are exceptions to that binary. People who are intersex have value in and of themselves. Let's be clear about that. At the same time, the medical conditions that are reflected here do not create a continuum of sex and gender so much as they remind us of how sexuality and gender were intended to be expressed and experienced—that there is a true north. This should help form Christian convictions about normative experiences but should not be wielded as a weapon against others. Hold this with humility, engage others with civility, and pray that you might have more compassion for those whose experience is a departure from your own.

Likewise, when we consider gender identity, we recognize that some people do not experience themselves as the gender that corresponds to their biological sex. A biological male may not experience himself as a boy; a biological female may not experience herself as a girl.[2]

Reasons for Discordant Gender Identity

At present, we don't have identifiable reasons for the experience of discordant gender identities. This experience is similar to intersex, but it is also different in important ways. Without having a definitive cause of discordant gender identity in the way we have definitive medical conditions that cause intersex experiences, there is much speculation about what is happening, how to understand it, and how to respond.

I recognize that some readers will say we do have an identifiable reason for discordant gender identities: sin. The argument here would be that people, including teens today, do what they want, expressing themselves in rebellion against God's design. This line of reasoning may draw on Romans 1:24–27. Although people do indeed rebel against many sources of authority, including norms around sexuality and gender, I have found in my practice that young people often find themselves with an unwanted, discordant gender identity that causes distress. Their experience appears to be not an act of rebellion but a dawning and distressing realization of something unchosen. You might ask: Can discordant gender identities *ever* be an act of rebellion? Well, I suppose so. Nearly anything can become a stage upon which rebellion occurs. But the idea of choosing such an identity as an act of rebellion goes beyond what I have seen in practice. The fact that something *can* be a stage for rebellion doesn't mean that it *is* a stage for rebellion. I have suggested elsewhere[3] that young people are navigating changing language and categories of gender and gender identity in ways that their parents were never exposed to. We should help young people navigate the meaning-making and sense-making stories about gender that they are currently encountering. It is not particularly helpful to bring a charge against them based on our assumptions of their motivations.

I am sometimes asked if the pivot away from viewing discordant gender identity as personal sin or willful disobedience puts the Christian in a position to celebrate a continuum of genders. Here is what I would say: A Christian can recognize the binary of man/woman or boy/girl and also recognize that there are exceptions to that binary, just as we saw with intersex. These exceptions may very well be discussed as suggesting a continuum of genders, but that is not a claim a Christian needs to make. I am less drawn to the idea of a continuum of genders than to just acknowledging that exceptions to the binary exist. There may be an increased number of gender identities with which people align themselves—whether it makes sense to discuss these as a continuum or just a plethora is open for discussion—and these gender identities will likely continue to grow in number as language and categories change to encompass people's diverse experiences and ways of naming those experiences. (This dynamic is what we described as a looping effect in chapter 1.)

Gender and Child Development

The approach that has been most appealing to me is to provide a kind of scaffolding around children that recognizes their developmental stage of life, conveys the beliefs you want them to have, and reflects the values you hold as a Christian parent. As you incorporate the messages you convey about gender with a broader Christian vision for sexuality and sexual behavior, you will also want to foster the skills your child will need to navigate increasingly complex environments as they grow up.[4]

In discussions about gender, be prepared for teachable moments that come up from time to time. These are the unplanned moments in the day that become opportunities to share something about gender under the circumstances that have come up in that moment. The best way to plan for these is to have a kind of "working model" or "working theology" of sexuality and gender that you can apply to unplanned, unscripted moments, as these are the most common and potentially most impactful moments with your children.

- Your six-year-old son puts on his mom's high-heeled shoes and says, "Look, Mom! I'm wearing high-heeled shoes like you do!"
- One of your favorite television shows breaks to a commercial with a transgender girl and her parents and underscores the importance of hair care during her transition.[5]
- Your pizza delivery driver comes to the door and hands you and your son your pizza. The driver happens to be transgender.
- One of your favorite reality TV shows to watch as a family features a transgender contestant this season.[6]

Be intentional about what you model and teach your children. It may make sense to organize your response to various circumstances around the three Cs we've been discussing in each chapter: convictions, civility, and compassion. I could imagine that some unplanned moments will call for you to speak to your convictions more, while others may call for more civility or compassion.

Teachable moments about gender will also vary based on your child's developmental stage in life. You will say different things to your child based on their age.

Provide young children language for gender (boy or girl) and teach them that their gender is a reflection of their sex (male or female). As children age, it will be important that they understand that while there are norms for sex and gender, there are also exceptions. Some people experience their gender identity as in between or outside of the binary. Because of this, though most people use he/him/his and she/her/hers pronouns, others may prefer they/them because of how they experience their gender.

If you wonder whether your child may be experiencing their gender in a way that is different from the norm, we will discuss that in chapter 7. If you want to know how to help your older child or teenager respond to a friend from school who has transitioned, we will discuss those ideas in chapters 5 and 6.

When we talk with our kids about sexuality and gender, especially as we recognize variations such as gender discordance and various gender identities, it is important not to disparage people who have intersex conditions or experience a transgender or other-gender identity. The experience of a discordant gender identity is not something a person chooses. It is not a matter of being willfully disobedient. A young person sometimes *finds themselves* with a different kind of experience of their gender. They will have to figure out what to do about it and how to respond to this discordant gender identity, and we want to position ourselves next to them, to come alongside them rather than denounce them.

I encourage you to tell your child that you're excited that God made them a girl or a boy. Offer unconditional love for your child and use spontaneous moments to reaffirm your child, their gender, and God's intention from the creation stories to make us male and female. This is an important affirmation and one that parents should offer gladly and generously.

In some rare instances, this praise and unconditional love could be met with questions or feelings that are hard for a child to put into words. A child who experiences their gender as not aligning with their biological sex will find such praise confusing over time. Some children who experience this lack of alignment don't say or do anything with their vague feelings of discontent. Other children may try to express their discontent and lack of alignment through behaviors (e.g., wearing a towel as a dress) or questions (e.g., "When am I going to have breasts like you have breasts?") or statements (e.g., praying that God would make them a girl). Again, this is something we will return to in chapter 7.

Bringing the Conversation Home

I interviewed the parents of three children, two boys and a girl, ages sixteen, fifteen, and eleven. About three years prior to the interview, their uncle had transitioned. In the year prior to the more formal social transition, the parents noticed changes in the uncle's appearance, and they suspected that their kids would have noticed too. One day when the mom was picking up the kids from school, she turned around and said, "You may have noticed that your uncle has been dressing a little differently. Have you noticed this?" The kids said that they had but hadn't thought much about it one way or another. Mom went on: "Well, your uncle would now like to be called Ava. I want you to know that we love everyone, whoever they are, whoever they want to be. We love them for who they are, and that's just what we do." This wasn't the only conversation, nor was it the last conversation, but the parents wanted to set a direction for their kids to lead with love for their family, even when family members had experiences they may not be familiar with or have answers to at the moment.

Similarly, I was interviewing a mother of two boys: one middle schooler and one high schooler. When I asked how she talks to her boys about relating to kids at school who are navigating gender identity questions, she talked about being intentional with them in conversations about sex and gender by pointing out that there are people who might experience themselves as the opposite gender and that they can experience God's love for them. She shared a little of the language she uses:

> I ask him, "What do you see? What do you hear? What do you hear being said at youth group?" He does see a lot of things that are close to bullying. He sees people not fitting neatly into being male or female. I try to help him become more aware of the environment, more aware of name calling, more aware of pronoun usage and just help him reflect more on how he feels when things are said. I ask, "How do you want to interact with your peers or in that situation?"

In addition to conversations you can plan and initiate, it's also important to be prepared for the more organic moments with your child, the unscripted exchanges and teachable moments that come up when you are out running errands, picking them up from school, watching a television show together, and so on. Let's look at an exchange between a parent and her eight-year-old daughter when they were watching a favorite reality show:

> Parent: From that opening interview, it sounds like one contestant identifies as transgender. Do you know what that word means?
>
> Child: Well, yeah, I mean, I've heard the word, I guess.
>
> Parent: When you were born, we knew you were a girl. That's because we could see that God made you with a vagina, and that meant you had two X chromosomes in your cells, because that's what matches what females are. As you grew up, you learned what it meant to be a girl, and being a girl matched your chromosomes as a female. Well, when a person is transgender,

their experience of themselves as a boy or a girl doesn't match up with their chromosomes. They might have two X chromosomes in their cells like you did—so they are biologically female—but they grow up experiencing themselves as a boy. It looks like when we watched that interview, we were seeing someone who had an experience like that.

Child: Okay, so that's what transgender means? To be a different gender?

Parent: Yes, that's basically it. To experience your gender in a way that doesn't line up with your biology. For most people, the way they experience their gender matches their biology. That's true for you. That's true for me. It's true for most people you know. But for a small number of people, their experience of their gender does not match their biology. They experience themselves as a different gender than you would expect. Sometimes they feel like the other gender, so a male who experiences herself as a girl, or, in the case of the show we are watching, a female who experiences himself as a boy. Other times a person's gender may not quite fit boy or girl, and a person might have another word for what that's like for them.

The general idea is to be prepared for teachable moments by having a few definitions in place and ways that you might talk about gender and sex, gender identity, and transgender experiences. Don't put pressure on yourself to have all the conversations in one conversation. You can return to the topic in the future. Also, this is not so much a lecture to your child as it is a natural, organic conversation at a teachable moment.

Cultural Ambassador: Our Three Cs

As we conclude this chapter on talking to your children about gender, the main convictions we've addressed have to do with beliefs about the relationship between our bodies and our gender. Most Christians hold a high view of the body and of how gender and gender identity are intended to correspond with the biological aspects of sex, such as chromosomes, gonads, and genitalia. Our bodies are not irrelevant, nor are they by happenstance. Our bodies are a part of creation, even when that creation is not always as it was intended. We can have that conviction while recognizing that there are people who do not experience their gender in the way most people experience their gender. Exceptions do not cast doubt on the norms; rather, exceptions point to the norms.

We can hold our convictions about sex and gender firmly and also be respectful of those who disagree. This is the civility part. It has to do with agreeing to disagree. If you are familiar with other perspectives, you can share your thoughts on them. I do that when asked, but I do not initiate conflict in these areas, nor do I disparage those who hold to other views. You will want to position yourself next to your child as they ask questions or as the topic comes up at school, on TV, or on social media. When I talk about being next to your child, think of it this way: If this was tennis, you would not be on the other side of the net playing against your child; rather, you would be on the same side of the net facing the challenge of a changing culture that may be confusing to them at times. You can be a resource who "thickens the plot" by responding thoughtfully to what is said at school, how the topic is covered in the news, and what is trending on social media. You can also be prepared to engage ideas and ask good questions to guide your child to greater nuance and insight without disparaging their views or the views held by their friends or others. If you mock people, that will say more about you than it will about the person you mock or the views that person holds. Being civil means remaining approachable, inquisitive, reasonable, thoughtful, and respectful.

Compassion again speaks to how we care for people whose experience of gender identity does not reflect what most people experience. We can be compassionate and respectful toward them and encourage others to interact with them in a similar manner. The person who experiences a discordant gender identity must navigate through competing worldviews and competing sets of assumptions about sex and gender and gender identity. Given the rise in alternative ways to think about norms and exceptions to norms, I suggest you take the time to learn about these alternatives and reflect on how you would like to respond. We want to position ourselves alongside the person asking these questions and learning about different perspectives. How we hold our views and relate to those around us who disagree will determine how open others are to listen when we share what we believe to be true.

5

What do I say when my child asks about someone in their class who has decided to transition?

Your son, age twelve, comes home from school one day and says that he has a classmate who plans to start using medications to keep him from going through puberty. Your son asks you what his friend could mean by that. Your son has been learning about puberty and the changes he can expect, and he is wondering why his friend is thinking about not going through puberty.

This chapter is about how to talk with your kids about the decision other people make to transition. In the case above, a friend at school is considering the use of hormone blockers that will keep him from going through puberty for a period of time, typically no more than one or two years. Technically, the use of hormone blockers is not transitioning; it is meant to be a kind of pause button on puberty, giving a child more time to explore gender identity before going through puberty.

However, while the use of puberty blockers is not transitioning, it has been strongly associated with the decision to transition eventually.[1] Puberty blockers were originally intended to help kids who went into puberty too early—what is referred to as "precocious puberty." For several years now, these blockers have been used by some professionals to buy time for an older child to explore their gender identity while not having to experience an unwanted puberty. This approach was first developed in the context of a comprehensive model that included considerable assessment, such that the decision to block puberty and eventually facilitate transition applied to only a small subset of children for whom gender dysphoria was thought to likely continue. Today, however, puberty blockers are much more common. With the rise in gender clinics in the U.S. and the diverse ways in which gender dysphoria and transgender experiences are evaluated, parents may be less confident that comprehensive evaluations are taking place; far more children pursue puberty blocking and transitioning now than did so when the approach was first developed.

Social or Medical Transition

If your son or daughter has a classmate who has decided to transition, you might take note of whether they are talking about a *social* transition or a *medical* transition. The case above describes the use of blockers, which may lead to a future medical transition through the use of cross-sex hormones. Medical transitions are less common than social transitions.

What is a social transition? A social transition is a shift toward presenting oneself as the other gender (or another gender). This is usually done through clothing and hairstyle, as well as a request that people refer to them by a different name and pronouns. A partial or informal social transition might happen with just close friends or people someone has met online, while a more formal social transition would be with everyone—parents, extended family, peer group, and so on. A more complete or formal social transition with a school-aged child or teen would typically be communicated to the school administration and be reflected in an expectation that teachers refer to the child by their chosen name and pronouns, a plan for the use of an appropriate bathroom, a plan for the use of appropriate shower and locker room, and so on.

Living as another gender is a difficult topic for Christians to navigate. Although there is diversity of thought about this among Christians, most conservative Christians do not commend living as another gender. They believe that people should live and present in a manner that corresponds to their biological sex, and this is what happens for the vast majority of people. Many Christians also believe that experiencing oneself and presenting oneself in a way that corresponds to one's biological makeup is a reflection of God's intention for gender at creation.

At the same time, Christians must recognize that in a fallen world, there may be instances when presenting oneself in ways that correspond to birth sex may be very painful and distressing for reasons we do not fully understand. We also must consider that some people who experience a discordant gender identity have said that presenting themselves in ways not typically aligned with their birth sex has helped them reduce distress and improve daily functioning. It is unclear how severe distress needs to be to warrant this kind of self-presentation. Some say that gender-atypical presentation should be supported when it is deemed a "medical necessity." Others would argue that any transition is unchristian regardless of the level of distress. Still others would say that a person's sense of gender identity is a reliable moral guide for self-presentation. In other words, anyone who desires to transition should transition. This is probably the view that is potentially most in conflict with a Christian worldview; Christians should have empathy for this condition, but it's hard to see how treating gender identity simply as a means to self-fulfillment aligns with the Bible's vision for gender.

Teachable Moments

As we discussed in the previous chapter, it's important to be prepared for the organic teachable moments that will come up with your child. I was interviewing a mother of a high school boy who admitted to me that her son hasn't yet talked with her about a friend or acquaintance who is weighing whether to transition, although he does have some friends and acquaintances in this circumstance. When I asked what she would hope to communicate to her son if the conversation were to come up, she shared:

> I'd like to land more toward questions and invite my son to think through it: "What do you imagine your friend is experiencing and how much is he carrying that would lead him to facing those kinds of decisions?" I'd like to help my son step more into the nuance of that experience. "What do you think your friend may be needing or wanting from you? Have they been able to share with their youth group or minister? How could you be an advocate for your friend?" Those kinds of questions.

I also spoke with parents whose son was friends with a girl who had a short haircut and had begun dressing differently; the friend had just asked their son to use he/his/him pronouns. (We will come back to the topic of pronouns a little later in a subsequent chapter.) The mother asked her son, "How did the conversation come up?" Her son shared a little more about the conversation they had that day at the lunch table. The mother asked, "Is he still going by the same name or a different name?" She also asked, "Do the parents know?" The friend's parents did know, and the parents I interviewed were intentional about checking in with the friend's parents, trying to anticipate how they might support the family. When the friend came over to hang out, the mother asked her son, "What can you do for your friend? Would he want a more formal acknowledgment of the changes he is making? Maybe have a few friends over and show support in that way?" When the friend came over, the mother was intentional about staying curious and asking questions such as, "What will you have on your middle school graduation diploma? Are you thinking of making a formal name change or something less formal?"

The parents shared that these kinds of conversations set a good tone of genuine interest. They noted that their son's friend didn't have answers to some questions—the friend was on a bit of a journey, taking things as they came. Their son's friend and his parents appreciated the posture they took of coming alongside them and being available to them rather than pulling away. Later, when they learned that some of their son's friend's peers had pulled away from him, they hosted an event at their cottage and had a getaway with peers who were able to find ways to support their son's friend. The event set in motion a different social dynamic that was more supportive and inclusive, a dynamic that continues to this day.

What if the friend had been a Christian? Would I suggest doing anything differently? I don't think I would. Other questions would arise, of course, about how their faith informed their decision-making. If they felt they could share that, it could be informative to learn more about how they see themselves bringing together their Christian faith with their response to gender discordance. I am saying in part that I am not sure that there is one Christian response to all experiences of gender dysphoria. That would seem to me to be too rigid for the range of experiences that might be before us. Rather, I think we help people manage their dysphoria as best they are able this side of eternity. If they can do that without transitioning, then I think that is the least complicated path. (In my previous writing, I discuss coping with dysphoria in the least invasive way possible.[2]) Could there be cases in which I would recommend giving additional steps greater consideration, even if the person was a Christian? I think so, particularly if the concern was considered life threatening (in terms of risk of suicide) or if the step was deemed medically necessary.

Bringing the Conversation Home

Let's return to the opening vignette about your son's classmate at school who is thinking about using puberty blockers. How would you respond to your son who asks you about this classmate?

Keep in mind that you are raising your son to live with purpose as a Christian in relation to others in his life. We do not want to assume this other child and his family are not Christians simply because they are considering the use of blockers. We don't know whether they are believers or not. We don't really know anything about them from this vignette other than that the child is looking at delaying puberty.

Here is a sample dialogue between a father and son that could be informative and open up a discussion:

> Son: There is a friend from school who is talking about taking something that will mean he won't go through puberty. I'm not really sure why.
>
> Dad: He may be transgender or experiencing gender dysphoria. There are actually medications available today to stop people from going into puberty. These medications were first developed to help children who were going into puberty really, really early. That's called precocious puberty. But since your friend is your age and not eight or nine, this is not precocious puberty.

Son: Oh, okay. So why would he not want to go through puberty?

Dad: People delay puberty for different reasons. It might be because he is experiencing gender dysphoria and may fear that puberty will be really, really difficult for him, so he could be using blockers to push back the decision whether to actually go through puberty as a boy or whether to consider other steps that might help him.

Son: What do you mean by gender dysphoria? Why would puberty be any worse for him than it is for other guys?

Dad: Gender dysphoria is the experience of distress or unpleasant feelings that can come up when a person's gender identity as a boy or a girl doesn't match their biological sex as a male or female. When a person—maybe like this person at school—experiences gender dysphoria or these unpleasant feelings, they may have very strong feelings of concern as they think about going through puberty. They worry that going through puberty could make those unpleasant feelings that much worse.

Son: How would delaying puberty help? Doesn't he eventually have to go through puberty anyway?

Dad: That's a good point. Your friend will eventually go through puberty. What he might be trying to work out is whether to go through puberty as a boy. If he makes that decision, he would just stop using this medication and everything would resume as it would have before he got on the blockers. He could also decide to take cross-sex hormones, so estrogen, in his case. It would be a different kind of experience, but he might be thinking it could help his dysphoria.

Son: Would it help?

Dad: There are definitely people who say it would help because it has helped them. Some research on this has said that some of the people who have taken cross-sex hormones say they have been helped. Studies like that are tricky to understand. The fact that the family participated in the study at all, and that parents were supportive of the medical interventions, has to be taken into consideration too.

Son: Okay, so it can be helpful for some people.

Dad: I think so. There are some serious side effects, however, and life-changing consequences, so it is a decision that a person really has to think through carefully. From what I understand, there also hasn't been that much research on the long-term use of these cross-sex hormones with teens your friend's age, so it may be hard to say what that will be like for your friend over a much longer period of time.

Son: That's wild.

Dad: I should also say that there have been people who took those steps but then a few years later regretted it and ended up reversing course, which is difficult, but it was what they felt was best for them. Your friend might want to be thoroughly evaluated by professionals who work with people who have had similar experiences to be sure that this is a better way to go than other ways.

Son: Okay, that's interesting. There's a lot to think about.

Dad: There is a lot for him and for his parents to think about, and I haven't really mentioned anything about how we as Christians might approach a decision like that.

Son: What do you mean?

Dad: Well, mostly what I told you is a kind of summary of what people have said has or has not been helpful. Whether something works or is helpful is important. But as Christians, we also look at what we think God would have us do in the circumstances we face. It's not just about utility or if something works. We also want to add a step into our decision-making process where we pray for wisdom and discernment about what God would have us do. We want to read the Bible to see if it says anything about this. We'd probably want to talk with our pastor or others we trust about this. Does that make sense?

Son: Yeah. I hadn't thought of that part. I guess I was thinking mostly about whether it really works.

Dad: That makes sense to me to think about it that way too. There are many things to weigh, and I hope we can be a good source of support to your classmate. I'm not sure what that will look like, but let's keep talking about it.

Cultural Ambassador: Our Three Cs

We've been discussing how you talk to your own child who knows a classmate or friend who has decided to transition. As we think about the three Cs of conviction, civility, and compassion, we want to model for our children how these three Cs coexist in the life of the Christian, especially in our relationship to those who are vulnerable and who are walking out a difficult path.

We have discussed our convictions about God's creational intent. Let me urge you not to weaponize these convictions. Do not model for your child and encourage your child to use their convictions in ways that are hurtful toward others. You and your child can hold convictions about gender without declaring these convictions in an antagonistic way. I think Christians should practice how to discuss their beliefs in a winsome manner. I would not recommend or model the position of simply disputing people you disagree with under the guise of standing up for what you believe in. Often, our kids' friends do not have the same theological reference points our own kids have, or the same reference points *we* have and want our kids to understand. Strong criticism of another person's decisions is likely to be misinterpreted as a kind of Christian antagonism toward them as a person; even if this is not what you intend to communicate, it could easily be interpreted that way. It is important to see the big picture here: *How do you want your Christian witness to be present in the life of this friend and his family?* Do you want your witness to be about your criticism, as though a theological declaration would point them toward Christ? Or do you want your witness to be about your presence?

If you were asked what you thought, you could always try to put your reservations into words. But I'd recommend doing even this with a lot of humility, admitting that you do not know what you would decide if you were faced with a similar decision, because none of us can be certain what we would do when we are not the ones facing a challenging real-world decision. Humility can take you far in these conversations.

Hold conviction and relate to others with civility and respect. Your child's friend has decided to transition. This is not the time to dispute them. Think about major decisions you have faced. Once you have made a decision, you are unlikely to welcome those who dispute you over the path you have chosen; you are much more likely at that point in the decision-making process to dig in your heels and reiterate all of the reasons why you have decided as you have. What do you want from those around you in those moments? You want them to listen to you, come to some understanding of your decision from your point of view, and offer to support you in some tangible way. You can do the same in situations like this one.

Providing support is not the same as indicating agreement. Agreement is saying, "I think you are doing what you should do under the circumstances. This is the right decision; this is the right direction." Support can mean watching the friend's siblings when they have an appointment, making meals, going for walks with one or both of the parents, allowing a parent to share their journey in greater detail, or just quietly praying for the family or praying for wisdom and for how God would want you to be present to the family. Each of these tangible expressions of support are not the same in my mind as agreeing with every decision a person makes. But these practical expressions convey the love of God for that person or family through your presence as you extend yourself toward the other. These are expressions of love.

Put differently, you can enrich the relationship by doing more than agreeing to disagree. You can demonstrate compassion— toward the friend, toward the process of decision-making, toward the journey they have been on and will be on for years to come.

6

How should I guide my child in their interactions with a transgender friend?

Your daughter comes home from high school and shares with you that she is not sure how to relate to a friend of hers who is trans. This friend is male and was always known as a boy throughout elementary and middle school, but in the shift to high school, he shared with her and with others at school that he is a girl. He has asked your daughter and other friends at school to refer to him not as Brian but as Brianna and to use *she* and *her* pronouns rather than *he* and *him*.

In this chapter we explore the question of guiding or coaching your child in their exchanges with a transgender friend. We want to look at what grace and truth could look like in these exchanges.

Difficult topics often bring up the question of how to balance grace and truth. Some simplistic applications of the grace-and-truth principle can amount to something like, "Be kind about it all, but make sure they know that they are wrong." This is not the angle of entry I recommend in our interactions with transgender people. It is not the approach I think you should encourage your teen to take with their friend who identifies as trans.

What does balancing grace and truth mean in this situation? What will it mean to have truth as a foundation and to extend grace to one another?

Truth

The *truth* part of the grace-and-truth balance is that traditional Christians believe that gender and gender identity were originally intended by God to correspond to one's biological sex. We see this not only in general revelation, through the scientific study of human biology and reproduction, but also in the special revelation of the stories of creation.

In most cases, this expectation of correspondence or concordance is exactly what happens. Males experience themselves as boys, and there are many ways to be a boy. Likewise, females experience themselves as girls, and there are many ways to be a girl.

However, we are seeing an increasing number of experiences that vary from this norm. Christians recognize that variations around gender do occur in nature, and insofar as that is true, we can agree with those around us about different experiences of gender identity. But when the Christian says that variations around gender occur in nature, we do not assume that nature is as it was originally intended. Rather, we know from our own experience that nature is fallen, that not everything experienced on this side of the fall is something we commend.

This is the *truth* part of grace and truth. But we can hold this truth with some humility, recognizing that this is a difficult topic, that gender discordance must be a difficult experience, and that there is much we don't understand about it. We can know things to be true but not know everything there is to know about a topic or how best to respond to it.

Grace

Recall the principle mentioned in the preface: Christians can point with the sword of truth.[1] We can point to what we believe to be true and stay in relationship with others who disagree with that truth. This is part of what it means to bring grace into the grace-and-truth equation. By bringing your sustained presence in the life of another, you make Christ present. You embody the love God has for the person. Pointing toward truth brings truth to the table, while staying in the relationship in meaningful and supportive ways brings grace to the table.

We can extend people grace by remembering that we haven't faced the same challenges and decisions they have faced. We want to come to a better understanding of the backstory that has shaped people into how we know them today. This is the grace part of the grace-and-truth balance. Christians know that we live in a fallen world, and we interact with people every day who do not see the world the way we do. They have different frames of reference for all kinds of things and experiences, and those who are not Christians may not understand our starting point in discussions of sexuality and gender.

Also, depending on how you think about gender, you may not be certain whether management of gender dysphoria is a moral concern, or if it is best understood as a way of coping with a very difficult situation. Perhaps management of gender dysphoria is meant to vary from person to person and might shift in the same person over time.

Our frame of reference as Christians is that we hope to trust God with all aspects of our lives, but we do that trusting in fits and starts. We make gains in some areas but struggle in others. We don't want to single out sexuality and gender; rather, we recognize that as Christians we all have areas in our own lives where we struggle to trust God as a good and loving Father. It could be our finances, our education, our work or career, our marriage, our parenting, and so on. A person's sexuality and gender is another area to trust God with—and if a person does not have a relationship with God, they would have no reason to even begin to explore what trusting God with that part of their life would look like. We want to enter into and maintain a relationship with our non-Christian friends in ways that make a relationship with God a more likely consideration. Perhaps we can inspire curiosity in our friends about what it means to know God personally and trust in him with all aspects of our lives.

We would not expect someone who does not know God as a good and loving Father to trust him with their gender.

We should also keep in mind that the way a person manages their dysphoria is not necessarily a reflection of their spiritual depth or sanctification. If we think of dysphoria as a medical condition a person experiences, then our conversations about the most helpful protocols for managing dysphoria are primarily medical rather than spiritual. We can recognize the concerns we have about different management strategies and whether they reflect God's best for that person, but that is different from assuming that some strategies are obviously a reflection of a less mature spiritual journey or one of disobedience to God's revealed will for this specific person.

In a recent consultation on gender, an older teen—a natal male who experiences themselves as female—shared that making a social transition had been helpful to her but challenging in conversations with her parents.

> Socially transitioning around my friends has been really helpful, and the next step for me, I feel, is taking it public. But it's been really tough trying to get my parents to understand, since I hid it from them for so long because I was very anxious about

losing their support. Coming out to them has been really good for our relationship and my trust in them, but it's been hard to get them to understand it in its whole.

There is a lot in this quote, but I want to highlight what a partial social transition with friends was like for this person. It had been "really helpful" as a kind of test of how people might respond to her presentation and how that could affect her. There is also more to experiences of gender than just how a person presents themselves or how they wish to be identified (with names and pronouns). That "more" is what I think the person above means when they say, "It's been hard to get [my parents] to understand it in its whole." This is where a friend can invite the person to further unpack their experience: what they are looking for from others, what understanding looks like, and what the "whole" of their experience of gender is like for them, including their physical discomfort, emotional discomfort, body image, and other aspects of their experience.

Do you recall the story we told in our last chapter about your son's friend who was thinking about using puberty blockers? Let's fast-forward and say your son is now fifteen; his classmate has elected to make a medical transition through the use of cross-sex hormones. This means that your son's classmate is now taking estrogen to feminize his appearance and redistribute fat, and he plans to continue down a path of medical transition. If he hasn't already, he will likely request that your son and others at school refer to him with female pronouns and possibly a new name. Your son's classmate will eventually experience breast development, the feminizing of his (now her) eyes and face, decreased thickness and rate of growth of hair on her body, and so on. She may also experience changes in the range of emotions she feels.

There is a chance, of course, that your son's friend has decided against a transition. For many reasons that are personal, reasons we may not be privy to, a person might decide not to initiate a medical transition. But, for our purposes, let's assume that your son's friend has made a social transition and is continuing down a path of medical transition.

Recall that your son has tried to be a source of support to his classmate for the past three years. What does your son's ongoing support for his classmate look like as this transition takes place? That will vary from situation to situation and depend on whether they are acquaintances or closer friends. In the paragraph above, I made a shift in pronouns to reflect how I could see your son electing to relate to his classmate; let me address that in more detail.

The Use of Pronouns

Your son might decide to demonstrate support for his friend by using the pronouns and name his friend requests. This can be a difficult decision for some families to navigate, and it can be hard to make this adjustment. But I tend to adjust the pronouns I use at transgender people's request in an effort to stay engaged in relationship with them. I have known people who have elected not to use the pronouns a transgender person requests; they have said that switching pronouns is not speaking the truth about who the person really is in terms of their chromosomal makeup. I can understand this position. However, I don't think your son's friend will hear truth in the decision not to use her pronouns; I think she will see your son as antagonistic and unsupportive. This will probably not point her to a different way of seeing things; more likely, it will solidify in her mind the belief that some people are for her while others are against her.

We want to move away from a for/against arrangement in our relationships. God is for people, and we are for this classmate. That's not the issue. But it is important to understand how our actions will be interpreted in this cultural context. What way of relating will allow us to stay in relationship with a person and point them to a far more important relationship with God as a good and loving Father? If we choose not to use the pronouns requested, I don't think it will point people to God in most cases. Rather, I suspect the relationship will end and there will be minimal if any contact in the months and years to come. The question is not whether to speak truth; the questions are: which truths will you prioritize speaking, how will you convey those truths, and when? You see, another truth is that God is a good and loving Father who wants a relationship with your son's classmate. That's why I'd stay engaged by using the classmate's chosen name and pronouns. I would continue to be invested in the relationship. I may or may not agree with every decision this person is currently making, plans to make, or will make in the years to come, but that's probably true for most people who are in relationship with one another. By being in relationship, I bring Christ to our exchanges. Most people find their way to Christ through the exchanges they have with people who bear the name of Christ: Christians or "little Christs." That's your son. That's you.

Bringing It Home

In an interview with a mother of a high school boy, I asked what she would want to say to her son about a friend who transitioned. She offered,

> I'd like to invite [my son], in light of his faith, to think about who he wants to be to his friend. I'd like him to consider, "Is it your job to correct or instruct? Or could your role be something different? Have you asked your friend what he needs from you? Could you encourage him in his faith?"

This is the kind of posture I am encouraging you to take as parents. How you think of your role or your child's role in the life of their friends will directly inform your angle of entry into a conversation that can be quite complex.

Let's return to the case study that opened this chapter. How do you coach your daughter, a freshman in high school, in her relationship with a longtime friend whom she has known for years as Brian, who now wants to be known as Brianna?

The only thing we know from the case as it was introduced is that your daughter's friend has changed her name and wishes to be known as Brianna. We will have to fill in a few more details, but for now, let's look at what we know and how you can respond.

There is a good opportunity here to ask your daughter what she thinks of what her friend has shared with her. Don't jump to the request about name and pronouns. Just ask her what she thinks and feels. How is she responding to her friend?

Parent: What do you think? How are you feeling about it?

Daughter: I don't know. I haven't given it much thought. It's just a strange thing to adjust to, but I guess it's a bigger adjustment for Brian . . . I mean, Brianna. That's going to take some getting used to, to be honest.

Parent: Well, as you think about it, maybe it's something we can come back to. I imagine it will be a journey rather than a one-time event. So there is time to sit with it and think about it.

Daughter: I appreciate that. I think you're right. A journey rather than an event. That's a good way to think about it. I've known Brian for years, but I have to say that I haven't really known what was going on with him. I can't really imagine, to be honest.

I could imagine a scenario where your daughter goes one of two directions over time in responding to her friend. One direction would be to accommodate her friend without any reference to the questions that arise for the Christian. What I would want to do as a parent is to "thicken the plot" around gender identity by asking her to think about and discuss with me a Christian perspective on gender—not to keep her from being supportive of her friend, but to help her ground her response in Christian considerations that balance grace and truth. I want her to remain in relationship with this friend and to be sympathetic to the friend's experience, but I also want her to see the weight of the decisions her friend has been facing, even if the friend has not shared that part of the journey with her.

Parent: It sounds like you are pretty comfortable with your friend's request.

Daughter: Yeah. I mean, it's different, it's an adjustment, but I know other trans kids and it's cool. It happens. I was just a little surprised with Brianna. I'm definitely going to support her.

Parent: One thing I've often admired about you is the loyalty you show to your friends. I think it is a great quality in you. What do you think it will mean to support Brianna?

Daughter: I don't know, but I could imagine some kids giving her a hard time. I'll lend my support. Tell them it's not cool to do that. Make sure they show respect.

Parent: It sounds like you want to have her back. I can appreciate that. I think one reason we have a friend's back is because they are made in God's image. We don't want them to be mistreated because God loves them and wants what's best for them. I think with transgender experiences, it can be hard at times to know what is best for a person.

Daughter: What is best for Brianna, is that what you mean?

Parent: Yes, discerning what is best for a person can be really difficult. There is a lot to consider. Is a social transition what's best? Would other approaches to gender identity be on the table? Those are tough questions to answer, and it can be hard to know what God would want in these situations, but that question of what God wants is also an important one for Christians to ask and pray about.

Daughter: Yeah, I don't know either. I guess I hadn't really thought about it. What I do know is that I want Brianna to feel safe at school and with me.

Parent: That makes sense to me. Sometimes feeling safe is what someone needs in order to weigh other decisions they are facing down the road.

The other direction your daughter could go would be to be overly critical of her friend or to reject her friend. That is also not a Christian response. I would want as a parent to "thicken the plot" around gender identity by asking my daughter what it means to relate to any other friend whose individual characteristics she is unfamiliar with. In other words, we assume your daughter has friends of different ethnic or racial backgrounds than her. She has friends who are not Christians—maybe agnostic or atheist or of another world religion. There are many, many individual and group characteristics that she does not share with friends, yet she has the ability to relate to them. I want her to reflect on that and bring those capacities to this friendship. I might talk about other friends she has grown close to over the years, friends who were different from her in meaningful ways, but the differences ended up being opportunities to learn more about the world around her.

Parent: It sounds like you are pretty uncomfortable with your friend's request.

Daughter: Yeah, I'm not sure what to do. I have other friends who are just not going to go there; they told me that already. They said Brian should know better than to expect everyone to acquiesce to him. That's kind of where I'm at too.

Parent: One thing I've often admired about you is that you want to think this through for yourself. If I can offer this: I've known people like Brian, people who have not experienced their gender in ways that fit with their body. They didn't choose to experience their gender in that way; they found themselves with those experiences and were trying to figure out what to do next. I wonder if that's true for your friend.

Daughter: Could be. I can't imagine Brian just choosing this to score points socially. It's not working out that way, I can tell you that. It's been kind of a nightmare for him.

Parent: I suspect that in the coming days and weeks, a lot of kids are going to be talking *about* Brian. It might be good to talk *to* him. Maybe it would be worth hearing directly from Brian what these experiences have been like for him. Perhaps hearing from him firsthand would be a place to start.

Daughter: People are definitely talking *about* Brian. That's
for sure. I like the way you put that, though.
It would make sense to connect with Brian directly about it all. That would probably help me
understand his desire to be known as Brianna.

A conversation like this one does not answer all the challenging questions your child may face, but there is something
appropriate and healthy about redirecting them to the person
that others may be talking about. There is also something appropriate and healthy about learning to guard against gossip
or growing close to one person at the expense of another. This
doesn't mean your child can't talk to you about Brian; you are
trying to be a sounding board and, more than a sounding board,
a source of wisdom, discernment, and prudence in relationships
and social circles that can be fraught.

Cultural Ambassador: Our Three Cs

This chapter has been about interactions you have as a parent
with your child when they tell you they have a transgender
friend at school. There will be a bit of overlap between the
application of our three Cs in this chapter and what we saw in
the previous chapter.

Recall that you are now modeling for your children how
to relate to others around a contentious and often polarizing
topic. You are modeling how to do this not just when they
approach an abstract topic in theory, but when they're facing
something seen and known and experienced by a friend. It is
important for your child to not demonize their friend. This
isn't just an issue; this is a real person in your child's life. Help
them understand Christian convictions without placing these
convictions in opposition to the friend or the friendship. Some
people might suggest that a Christian ought to have nothing to

do with someone navigating gender identity questions in their life. But the truth is the opposite: God loves this friend of your child. Hold convictions in a way that allows that love to come to the foreground. A balance of convictions and civility can do that, especially if your child sees you model compassion.

What are some practical ways to cultivate compassion? Think of God's heart toward those who are hurting and trying to find a way forward in their lives. Think about times you have faced hard decisions and did not know the right thing to do. Perhaps you have a lot of life experience and have been through the "school of hard knocks." Did God leave you in that place? I think most Christians look back on their lives—especially their toughest decisions and most challenging circumstances— and see better in hindsight the way God was at work. If you could go back and talk to your younger self, perhaps you could offer words of encouragement about how God is aware of your circumstances and wants you to draw close to him, teaching you to trust in his guidance and provision even if it isn't readily apparent. This is what it means to grow in faith. The only way to even get to a conversation like this with someone is to be in a relationship with them. If you invest in relationships with people, they might find through you that the God you worship is someone who motivates others to love and respect those around them.

If you believe you need to pull convictions to the foreground, you can also do that, but I would begin by emphasizing compassion. Once your compassion has been established, you can also recognize that Christians have convictions about the body and our embodied existence, and that the norms around gender and sex are not meant to be sources of pain but to be instructive of design. There may be rare instances that create the need to accommodate other experiences of gender identity, especially if a person's gender dysphoria is especially painful or life-threatening and such accommodations are deemed medically necessary. But even in these cases, which we might recognize exist only in a world touched by the fall, the creational norms for sex and gender are still true and meaningful for the vast majority of people. Departures from the norm do not mean that the norm is a source of oppression.

PART 3

What If Your Child Is Struggling with Gender Identity?

7

Are there any early signs that my child may be struggling with gender dysphoria?

Parents of a six-year-old boy came in for a parent consultation on gender identity. They shared that they noticed signs of gender atypicality in their son a year or more ago but did not think too much of it. As time has gone on, they have more questions about what is normal and how they should think about the behaviors they are seeing at home. For example, about four weeks ago, their son asked the mother when he will have breasts like she has breasts. A week before that, he had asked during bedtime prayers if God could make him a girl.

In this chapter we will learn about some of the signs that a child might be experiencing gender dysphoria. The challenge you will face as parents is that a lot of gender-related behaviors children engage in are pretty normal. For example, many boys might put on their mother's high-heeled shoes and walk around in them. It does not mean that a child has gender dysphoria. They could be just playing, seeking their mom's attention, or enjoying doing something they know their parents will set limits to. Similarly, a girl who enjoys rough and tumble play, who many might describe as a "tomboy," is not gender dysphoric by virtue of these preferences. She is playing and enjoying life within the broad range of ways girls encounter and enjoy the world around them.

In the case of the six-year-old boy who asked about getting breasts one day or prayed to be a girl, these behaviors are less typical. A more comprehensive assessment may help determine whether the diagnosis of Gender Dysphoria is warranted.

Before we jump into what gender dysphoria looks like in childhood and adolescence, I want to acknowledge that I will be drawing upon the *Diagnostic and Statistical Manual of Mental Disorders, 5th edition (DSM-5)* in describing the symptoms of Gender Dysphoria. You may not be familiar with the *DSM-5*, or you might wonder how much authority the *DSM* has when compared to the authority of the Bible. One way to answer this question is that the *DSM* is descriptive while biblical authority is prescriptive. In other words, the *DSM* helps us understand how people tend to experience the world—which experiences are normative for human beings today and which are outside the norm in important ways; the Bible, on the other hand, tells us *how* we are called to live in the context of these typical or atypical experiences. One result of the descriptive aspect of the *DSM* is that it provides some helpful, empirically based steps to understand and engage with different challenges. Just as psychology and psychiatry can provide helpful, evidence-based responses to complex issues like eating disorders or schizophrenia, so these fields can provide insights into the complex issue of gender dysphoria.

What Does Gender Dysphoria Look Like in Childhood?

There are a lot of factors involved in diagnosing children with Gender Dysphoria. According to the *DSM-5*, the diagnosis of

Gender Dysphoria in children refers to significant discordance between one's biological sex and one's gender that includes several criteria. A child has to display "a strong desire to be of the other gender or an insistence that one is the other gender." In addition, five of the following seven criteria also have to be met: a strong preference for the clothing of the other gender; a strong preference for the roles of the other gender in play; a strong preference for games and toys associated with the other gender; a strong preference to play with friends of the other gender; a strong rejection of the toys and games and interests associated with their gender; a strong dislike of their anatomy/genitalia; and a strong desire for the sex characteristics that would align with how they experience their gender.[1]

In order for experiences of gender dysphoria to warrant the diagnosis of Gender Dysphoria, the experiences have to be present for a minimum of six months and be associated with significant distress or difficulties in important areas of functioning, such as social or educational functioning.

Let's walk through each of these and provide a few examples. This is not to encourage you to diagnose your child, but to give you a better idea of what we see at our clinic and to give you an idea of when it might be helpful to pursue a professional assessment.

When the current diagnostic manual (the *DSM-5*) describes "a strong desire to be of the other gender or an insistence that one is the other gender," what does that mean? One example of this would be a girl who declares that she is a boy or that she wishes she were a boy, or who asks why God didn't make her a boy. This behavior alone does not warrant a diagnosis of Gender Dysphoria, but something along these lines would have to be present to warrant a diagnosis.

When the *DSM-5* describes "a strong preference for the clothing of the other gender," what does that look like? For a boy, he might show this by putting on his mom's high-heeled shoes, putting on a skirt or dress, or simulating a dress by putting a towel around his waist and saying, "I'm wearing a dress like you do, Mom!"

When we think about a strong preference for the roles taken by the other gender in play, what could that mean? One example is when kids play "house," and a girl routinely insists on being the dad or brother in the family. This can also be seen in strong preferences for certain gendered characters or avatars in games.

When the diagnostic manual mentions a strong preference for the toys and games associated with the other gender, what is it referring to? This can refer to a girl who has a strong preference for rough-and-tumble play, or a boy who demonstrates a strong preference for Barbies, dolls, or other stereotypical toys frequently played with by girls. Of course, the association of particular toys or games with one gender is steeped in stereotypes—and this behavior alone is not nearly enough to prompt a diagnosis of Gender Dysphoria. But sometimes stereotypical activities and interests reflect a person's identification as a boy or girl in our society today, and departures from these stereotypes—in tandem with other experiences—may reflect gender dysphoria, even though gender dysphoria is not reducible to a departure from stereotypes.

When we talk about a strong preference for friends of the other gender, what does that mean? We'll talk in the next chapter about a boy named Logan who prefers to play with his sister and her friends, all of whom are girls. This preference does not mean Logan has gender dysphoria, but it is a consideration if that preference is strong, not circumstantial (for example, the only kids in his neighborhood are girls), and extended over time. Similarly, if a young girl persistently rejects female playmates in favor of male playmates, that may be a consideration in determining whether she experiences dysphoria.

When we think about the rejection of toys and games often associated with their gender, what does that look like? This could be the boy who refuses to play games or be involved in activities that many boys show a preference for, such as Cops and Robbers, sports, or other activities. It could be the girl who rejects playing Barbies or house and is more interested in the activities the boys are playing.

When the diagnostic manual refers to a strong dislike of one's anatomy/genitalia, how might that be expressed? This could be the boy who asks God to take away his penis or fears growing body hair, and the girl who does not want her vagina or fears growing breasts.

When we think about a strong desire for the sex characteristics that would align with how they experience their gender, what does that mean? A boy might express a strong desire to develop breasts or grow long hair. A girl might wish she had a penis or could grow a beard. In other words, the boy has a strong desire for physical sex characteristics that correspond to how he experiences his gender (as a girl). Likewise, the girl wishes for physical sex characteristics that correspond to how she experiences her gender (as a boy).

Note that each of these criteria describes a "strong desire" or a "strong rejection." These criteria aren't describing occasional experiences or circumstantial preferences based on what is available to a child. They also go beyond a child's belief that there are social benefits to being the other gender. (For example, a girl saying, "Maybe they'd let me be in charge if I was a boy" probably isn't a sign of dysphoria.) Rather, when we think of "strong desire" and "strong rejection," these are established, significant, and enduring preferences. These strong preferences have to be present for a minimum of six months prior to making a diagnosis of Gender Dysphoria. A passing interest in Mom's clothing or various secondary sex characteristics is probably not a sign of dysphoria. These interests happen quite often. I would encourage you as a parent not to be anxious when your child expresses an interest that is gender atypical or otherwise falls outside of rigid gender stereotypes. This kind of thing is common and does not persist in most cases.

What Does Gender Dysphoria Look Like in the Teen Years?

The diagnosis of Gender Dysphoria in adolescents is the same as it is in adults. There are six criteria, and a teenager has to meet two of the six. The criteria are: discordance between how a person experiences their gender and their primary and/or secondary sex characteristics; a strong desire to no longer have their primary and/or secondary sex characteristics; a strong desire for the sex characteristics of the other gender; "a strong desire to be the other gender"; a strong desire to be responded to by others as the other gender; and an insistence that they have the typical responses or feelings of the other gender.[2]

As we did with childhood experiences of gender dysphoria, let's look at these six criteria. The first criterion has to do with significant discordance between how a teenager experiences their gender (which is their gender identity) and their primary sex characteristics (such as penis for males, vagina for females) and/or their secondary sex characteristics (such as facial hair or voice deepening for males or breast development for females). For teens who are just beginning to go through puberty, the discordance could be with respect to anticipated changes in puberty.

When the DSM-5 references "no longer wanting the primary and/or secondary sex characteristics they have," it is referring to the desire to have facial or body hair removal (for natal males) or the desire to have breast removal (for natal females). ("Natal" here refers to a person's birth: A natal female is someone born female.) Again, if a teen is younger, they could be voicing a desire to prevent the development of secondary sex characteristics.

The next criterion is to want the sex characteristics of the other gender. This could include a strong desire for breasts or rounder hips (for natal males) or a strong desire for greater muscle mass or facial hair (among natal females).

Another criterion is the strong desire to be of the other gender (or an alternative gender). The natal male who demonstrates a significant desire to be a girl and the natal female who expresses a significant desire to be a boy are included here. Either a natal male or a natal female could also express a significant desire to be gender nonbinary—for example, they might describe themselves as bigender, graygender, or pangender.

The next criterion for the diagnosis of Gender Dysphoria is to want to be responded to by others as the other gender (or, again, another gender such as nonbinary). This would refer to the natal male who wishes to be treated as a girl or the natal female who wishes to be treated as a boy.

Finally, the last criterion refers to an insistence that they have the typical responses or feelings of the other gender (or another gender other than the gender that corresponds to their natal sex). A natal male will hold with certainty that their feelings and reactions are those of a girl; likewise, a natal female will be certain that their feelings and reactions are those of a boy.

As we saw with the diagnosis criteria for children, the language of "strong desire" is meant to suggest a strong preference sustained over time. This significant, established, enduring preference must last for a minimum of six months prior to making the diagnosis.

In order to meet criteria for the diagnosis of Gender Dysphoria, the condition must also be associated with significant distress to the teen, or it must impair them in an important area, such as social or educational functioning.

Perhaps the most significant difference in a teen's experience compared to a child's experience is that a teenager can more directly communicate their experience of their gender. They can talk with you about how they experience themselves as the other gender and what that means to them. They can share their response to their primary and/or secondary sex characteristics, including a desire to no longer have those primary and/or secondary sex characteristics, just as they can share their desire for the primary and/or secondary sex characteristics of the other gender.

The gender dysphoria a teenager feels could have been present since they were a child, in which case it would be considered "early onset" (originating prior to puberty). Alternatively, the gender dysphoria may have only been present at or after puberty, in which case it would be referred to as "late onset" gender dysphoria.

As the criteria suggest, the anticipation of or experience of puberty can be especially distressing to a teenager with gender dysphoria. Puberty underscores sex differences in ways that can either help consolidate a person's gender identity with their natal sex or exacerbate existing distress about the discordance between their gender identity and their natal sex.

Teens may turn to various strategies to manage their gender dysphoria. Common strategies involve changing their length of hair (longer for natal males, shorter for natal females), making different clothing choices (androgynous or feminine-looking attire for natal males, androgynous or masculine-looking attire for natal females), changing their preferred name and pronouns, and using baggy clothing, long pants, and/or long-sleeved shirts to avoid seeing one's body shape or body hair.

A young adult we met with for a gender consultation shared their recollection of what was apparently gender dysphoria and how it was tied to shame—a sense that something was fundamentally wrong with them and that they were responsible for it:

> I always felt there was something fundamentally wrong about me. I misapplied early Sunday school lessons about how "people

do bad things" and thought, *I am an affront to God.* I can recognize this now as absurd but still struggle to shake that feeling of wrongness and shame. I remember worrying that people would "find out what I really was underneath the good kid." I think this was caused by shame. . . . I'm not sure if this was reflective of my gender dysphoria.

In this case, you can see how Christianity was complicated for this person. Basic Christian teaching about sinful behavior in general (that people do bad things) was internalized in a shame-based way. This is not uncommon among the people we have met over the years. Messages about transgender people in particular can be even sharper and more derogatory in ways that can also be internalized. The desire to hide oneself from others is also common—keeping others at arm's length is a frequent coping response for people who experience gender incongruence, reflecting their concern that if people knew about their experience of gender, they would be rejected.

Another young adult we met with reflected on her struggles with gender dysphoria and suicidal ideation, which she experienced when she was a teen:

> I didn't know how to tell people I wasn't okay, and [I] regularly thought about killing myself. I didn't want to, but I thought about it every day. I fantasized about how I'd do it, where, and how people would react. I thought that they'd understand that when I said I was dying inside, it wasn't hyperbole for normal high school stress. I didn't communicate this to my parents because I didn't know how, and didn't want to disappoint them.

Tragically, thoughts about killing oneself and attempted suicide are more common among people who experience gender dysphoria or have transgender experiences. We have also seen this among Christians navigating gender identity and faith.[3] Although gender dysphoria can differ in severity from one person to another, it can also fluctuate in severity for the same person in ways that can be quite distressing. It is no wonder people turn to creative means to manage their dysphoria.

Bringing It Home

Let's look at a common experience parents may encounter when raising young children. In the following exchange, we want to consider how a parent could be less reactive to a child who is displaying behavior that may concern many parents.

Son: "Mom! I have long hair like yours!"

Mom: "I was wondering where my bath towel went; it looks like you found it. Thank you!"

Son: "I have longer hair than you do!"

Mom: "I see you have my towel wrapped around your head. So that is your long hair?"

Son: "Yes! It is super long and beautiful."

Mom: "I see. Well, when you are done, please put my towel back in the hamper; I thought I put it there, but apparently I didn't."

Son: "Okay. But can I play with it for a little longer?"

Mom: "Well, since that towel is a little damp, why don't I find you something else you can play with?"

Son: "Okay, but it has to be really long like this towel, or my hair is going to be too short."

Mom: "Here is an older towel, and this one is dry. You like pretending you have longer hair?"

Son: "Yeah, it's long like your hair."

Mom: "What do you like about long hair?"

Son: "I guess it looks really pretty. Your hair always looks so pretty. I guess it looks pretty like your hair."

Mom: "Aww, that's nice of you to say. My long hair takes a lot of work to get it to look nice. I wish it didn't take Mommy quite so long to get it the way I want it. I think Dad wishes it didn't take that long either. Hey, I am going to make us some breakfast. I was thinking pancakes. When you are done, please drop the towel in the play box in your room and come down to eat."

Son: "Okay."

This mom is displaying a calm, secure parenting style that is nonreactive to her son's interest in longer hair. By nonreactive, I mean that she is responding to her son, but she is not reacting to his interest out of anxiety or fear about what it could mean. A fear-based response would be an overreaction to common play that happens from time to time. If this play persists and her son is saying or doing many other similar things, we might take a closer look at what this play means to the child. But we don't want the parents to overreact or to respond out of fear or anxiety, as this could be really shaming to a young child.

In most cases, a boy who plays like this with a towel will lose interest in doing so over time. One benefit to remaining calm rather than parenting out of fear is that, in all likelihood, there is nothing significant to the play, so overreacting to it would not be good use of energy and could shift the quality of the relationship with a child; the boy simply found something to do and was playing in a creative manner that likely wouldn't hold his attention that much longer.

In cases of true gender dysphoria, such play can be an attempt on the boy's part to communicate something to his mom.

He may be trying to tell her he does not feel like a boy or that he's not comfortable in his body. He may be trying to tell her that he feels more like a girl. One way to express this is to mimic something that seems distinct about being a girl and "express himself" in that way. The towel becomes long hair and a path for identification with his mom.

The same activity could carry two very different meanings. In all likelihood, this activity will not signal gender dysphoria. If the play persists even with redirection, and there are other signs of gender dysphoria that persist for more than six months, it does signal gender dysphoria. We will have a better sense of whether dysphoria is present over time, as we listen to other ways your child may be trying to speak to you about their experience.

Cultural Ambassador: Our Three Cs

As we have been looking at possible early signs that your own child may be experiencing gender dysphoria, I want to close this chapter by applying our three Cs to that kind of scenario.

As a parent, you have convictions about God's original intent for gender and sexuality. You have been teaching these convictions to your child, instilling certain beliefs in your child, affirming your child as a boy or a girl. You have been doing this—however imperfectly—out of your own convictions as a Christian.

If your child were to show signs of possible gender dysphoria, I would not want you to double down on your convictions by relying on gender stereotypes about boys and girls and insisting that those stereotypes must be displayed by your child. This approach would be the kind of fear-based parenting response that we are trying to avoid. Emphasizing gender stereotypes and attempting to press your child into that mold will create a lot of unnecessary stress and expectations for your child. They may attempt to comply, but it will not really be helpful to them. In fact, I think it can be harmful. It teaches your child that your love for them is conditional on displays of gender that may feel to them like a mask they put on or a role they play.

Do not allow your parenting to be driven by fear. When you identify your fears, find people you can talk to about those fears so your fears don't come out sideways in your parenting. I haven't known a parent who looked back on their parenting and said that their best parenting took place when they were especially anxious or fearful.

The compassion you show toward your child will be critical. Let them know that you love them, and affirm them in as many ways as you can. Even if you are considering the very real possibility that your child experiences gender dysphoria, try to have a couple of outlets for those concerns—friends or mentors you can discuss and process your fears with. Perhaps meeting with a counselor could be helpful. Ultimately, you want to be able to communicate your unconditional love for your child. That doesn't mean you won't be thoughtful and discerning about how you respond to your child's interests and expressions, but it means that in terms of the bigger picture, you are able to remain calm, communicate your love for your child, and take the appropriate steps to parent with some supportive boundaries around their experience and expression of gender identity.[4]

8

How can I help my child who is struggling with dysphoria?

Nate and Vicki, who are parents of a seven-year-old boy, came to our clinic for a parent consultation. They shared that about two years ago, they first saw signs of gender atypical behavior and interests. Their son, Logan, while playing a game with his sisters, asked to wear a dress outside, which was a little bit of a departure from their regular dress-up play. In the last eight months or so, Logan has verbally expressed wanting to be a girl. Two months prior to the consultation, Logan had put on a dress and tights and declared to his mother, "I'm a girl!" Later that night, when Vicki was putting Logan to bed, he said through some tears, "I wish God made me a girl." Much of what the parents identified as atypical behavior had to do with clothing and hair. For example, Logan had put a towel around his head and said with some enthusiasm to Vicki, "I've got long hair like yours!"[1]

If your own child were to struggle with gender dysphoria, what would you do? That might be a hard question to answer as a hypothetical if you are not dealing with the day-to-day reality of gender dysphoria. Negotiating the reality of gender dysphoria and actually responding is much more challenging than most people suppose.

Patience

Let's consider, however, what steps you might take. What *should* you do? We have found it helpful for parents to show some patience with their child's gender identity.[2] By patience I'm thinking of not trying to rush a quick resolution. Continue to express your unconditional love to your child, do not over-react, and try as best you can to slow down instead of rushing to a quick resolution. For example, when Logan picked out a doll for himself from a box of hand-me-downs, his parents did not make him put it back and pick something else. When Logan began sleeping with the doll in his bed each night, his parents again did not raise any objections. They did set limits, however. They made a rule that Logan's doll must stay at home when they went out to the store. They made this same rule for their daughter. They did not shame or embarrass Logan for his interest in dolls, but they did try to find ways to set boundaries that were applied consistently for all their children.

Ask any parent and you will find that they are constantly interacting with and responding to each of their children's different interests, statements, and mannerisms. When gender dysphoria is present, a child may be fairly consistent in expressing gender atypical interests and behaviors, and this can wear on a parent. I have seen many couples in which one parent is more frequently home with their child and is "on the front lines" in responding to the child's manifestations of dysphoria. This at-home parent may feel depleted from the number of requests their child makes (for example, to play with items they've been asked not to play with, or to wear clothing they have been asked not to dress up in). Often the parent who is not on the front lines has a stronger opinion about what should be allowed but is more detached from the day-to-day reality of their child's interests, requests, and emotions. This can lead to some strain between parents.

Strain between parents can also be fed by unrealistic expectations for the parent who is with their child most often, as if they should somehow do something that would resolve the child's gender-atypical behavior. In my experience, that just isn't going to happen if gender dysphoria is present. I've seen parents try to force an outcome for their child, but this has not generally proven effective—in fact, it may end up conveying to your child that they aren't good enough as they are. It can quickly create a set of expectations that your child feels they must measure up to in order to be accepted.

In Nate and Vicki's case, when a family with a young boy about Logan's age moved into their neighborhood, Vicki told Logan about the family, particularly the little boy, and asked Logan if he wanted to meet him. Logan declined, which, again, was okay. Nate and Vicki did not feel a need to force friendships with other boys onto Logan. Nor did they feel a need to limit Logan's play time with his sister and her friends. Those kinds of steps would have likely reflected a fear-based way of parenting (fear that Logan could be gay or transgender) and would likely be experienced by Logan as shaming. I could easily imagine Logan wondering what his parents thought of him and whether they disapproved of him and his interests. Vicki and Nate could continue to create opportunities for friendships with other boys as they came up organically, while refusing to overreact to Logan's preferences or force their son into relationships or activities that he chose not to pursue.

My experience has been that parents of young children are most helpful when they are nonreactive, emotionally even-keeled, warm, supportive, and able to communicate through words and behaviors their unconditional love for their child. There could be times to set limits, of course, or to redirect their child. But these moments need not be emotionally charged or fear-based, nor should they put their child at risk of feeling ashamed.

Reducing Fear

So far we have discussed being patient with your child's gender expression and identity. I have also suggested avoiding a fear-based approach to parenting. What do I mean by this? Parents often have fears about what their child's behavior could mean. I have found that when parents parent their child in reaction to those fears, they end up having regrets. Sometimes fear-based parenting comes across as anger or intensity that is hard for a child to understand as anything other than criticism. The more intense a parent's exchanges with their child, the more potentially injurious to the child. Most parents do not look back on their life and say that their best parenting took place when they parented out of fear.

For Vicki and Nate, reducing fear-based ways of parenting meant creating space for Vicki and Nate to articulate their fears. It helped to have them say those fears out loud to me and to each other. Vicki and Nate also had two close couple friends they could talk to. But they themselves did not have supportive parents. In fact, it was the grandparents on one side of the family, the ones who lived close by, who posed the greatest threat to reducing fear because of the things they said to Vicki and the way they criticized her parenting.

I've been discussing the experience of seven-year-old Logan and his parents, but what if you are parents of an older child or a teenager?

What If My Child Is a Teenager?

If your child is a teenager, you may be aware that they are different from other boys or girls their age. They may have been experiencing gender dysphoria for many years, perhaps since age four or five; this is referred to as "early-onset gender dysphoria." Most parents of teens with early-onset gender dysphoria are not surprised to know there is a term for their child's experience, though they may not know what that term is. But they know that it isn't just a phase their child is going through, because it has been a longstanding experience. Even if they don't fully understand what's going on, they probably at least understand that this experience isn't something their child is making up or choosing out of rebellion. However, there is an exception to this general rule: When a child learns that their gender expression is not approved by their parents or others, they may try to hide it to avoid punishment. In these instances, the gender dysphoria likely hasn't gone away; rather, it has been kept under wraps in an attempt to reduce conflict. In these cases, a child may have early-onset dysphoria even without their parents or others knowing about it.

In contrast, some parents reading this have teenagers who only recently shared that they are transgender or that they experience gender dysphoria. If they truly are experiencing gender dysphoria, it would be "late onset": gender dysphoria that is first experienced at or after puberty. While all experiences of dysphoria are challenging, late onset can be especially challenging because it is such a surprise, seeming to come out of nowhere. Many parents feel totally blindsided and have no real sense for what to do.

The first thing you can do is foster the kind of relationship with your teen that will help them be more comfortable sharing this part of their life with you. One sixteen-year-old we met with for a consultation shared about the fear she felt before talking to her father about her experience: "I was scared. I was so scared that my dad would kick me out, among other things. I lived my life from then [on] in sorrow and terror that no one will know how I feel until I can escape home."

A similar theme can be seen in a young adult who shared about her experience in high school as she considered opening up more to her family:

> I hit a point between my junior and senior year of high school where I thought about coming out but realized I wouldn't have much support. Even if I could guarantee full, unwavering support from my family (which I couldn't), I didn't have enough people at school who I trusted to feel safe coming out to. When I realized that, I just sort of buried the notion and kept my head down through senior year.

The second thing to do is to listen to your teenager as they share with you about their gender dysphoria. They might not phrase it that way; they might instead talk about being transgender. These are not the same thing, but they are related. Regardless of what language your teen uses to describe their experience, listen to them share about that experience, when it started, what it has been like, how they have responded to it so far, and things like that. Just listen. This is not the time to dispute what they are saying, and it's certainly not the time to tell them they are making it up or that it is all in their head or that it's because they are friends with so-and-so. Just listen. Tell them you love them. Tell them you are glad that they felt they could tell you about it. Tell them you will need time to learn more about what they are describing.

Many parents react in disbelief. They just don't think a person can experience their gender this way. I don't think this reaction is helpful. It positions you in opposition to your teen, and your disbelief will likely be interpreted in ways you did not intend.

Other parents react not in disbelief but with a kind of scrutiny, certain that what their teen is calling "gender dysphoria" or "being transgender" is really a social fad, a reaction to a peer group, or something along those lines. This raises a very complicated topic: the increase of late-onset gender dysphoria cases in recent years, and the theories some people have about how peer group influences have contributed to this increase. I'm not saying that social influence could never be a factor in a person's experience of gender, but I am advising against telling your child that this must be what has happened to them. If you as a parent decide this is what happened and declare it to your child—disputing their account—you will likely put yourself and your teen in an adversarial posture toward each other, a posture that will not be helpful in the weeks and months ahead.

Other parents react out of fears they have for the future. It is not uncommon to think of a "worst-case" scenario and react in an effort to avoid that scenario. As we've already discussed, fear-based parenting is unhelpful to you and to your teen. Many parents' fear has to do with medical transitioning—the lifelong use of cross-sex hormones that can jeopardize fertility, or the use of gender confirmation surgeries on otherwise healthy tissue. I'd encourage you to resist the impulse to dwell on these fears, even if your teen is describing these options or asking about them.

Assessment

It may be helpful to complete an assessment to help determine whether what your teen is experiencing is gender dysphoria. An increasing number of clinics specialize in this area, although it would be wise to find a referral to a person or clinic where competent, balanced assessment takes place. Some of your concerns about possible peer group influences could be looked at further. Also, there are several experiences that can look like gender dysphoria that are not gender dysphoria, so it can be helpful to determine what is going on. Clinics vary in quality. Some Christian clinics may not have as many staff who work in the area of gender, while some specialty gender clinics may not work as well with conventionally religious families or could even focus so much on affirmation that they fail to offer a more comprehensive assessment.[3]

There are conditions that are more commonly seen among people with gender dysphoria, so these can also be assessed. I'm thinking here of Autism Spectrum Disorder (ASD). While there does appear to be a relationship between ASD and gender dysphoria, it isn't clear what that relationship is. It can be helpful to have an evaluation for both of these conditions and to work with specialists in both areas who can communicate with one another in developing a proper plan for care.

It can also be helpful to prioritize care. If the proper diagnosis is Gender Dysphoria, there may be co-occurring concerns that are also important to address, concerns such as depression or anxiety. Co-occurring concerns would typically be addressed first, so that your teenager isn't making decisions about gender identity and dysphoria out of a depressed or anxious mood state.

Once a proper assessment has taken place and you've been able to determine whether the diagnosis of Gender Dysphoria is warranted, whether there are co-occurring concerns, and in what order to address them, you may return to the question of how to respond to gender dysphoria. At this point, I would encourage you to take a measured, stepwise approach where you try different ways of managing dysphoria to determine how helpful those steps are. This will probably be more helpful than simply passing your teen along to the next provider for medical care. Whether you are the parent of a child or a teenager, I suggest not thinking of gender as a train your child gets on where the inevitable destination is a complete medical transition.[4] I mentioned earlier that most transgender adults don't report using hormone treatment or gender confirmation surgeries, so medical interventions should certainly not be viewed as a destination everyone is moving toward.

Plateaus

One analogy I have used elsewhere is a shift from "mountain-top thinking" to "plateau thinking." When a child or teen receives the diagnosis of Gender Dysphoria, they are sometimes encouraged—by entertainment, on social media, and even in the mental health field to some extent—to think of medical transition as a mountaintop experience they should aspire to. In reality, a more common outcome among younger children is that their gender dysphoria could dissipate as they go through puberty. If dysphoria doesn't abate on its own, then the child (now in late adolescence) will likely find ways to manage their dysphoria: these strategies for management can be thought of along a continuum from "least invasive" (clothing and hairstyle preferences) to "most invasive" (hormone treatment and gender confirmation surgeries). Each strategy functions as a kind of "plateau": a comfortable landing place where a person can live in a healthy way for the long term. Most people appear to find a comfortable, livable plateau rather than reach the "mountaintop" of complete surgical transition.

What are common plateaus? I mentioned a few above, but here are several:

- Changes in hairstyle, such as keeping hair shorter or growing it longer
- Changes in outward clothing, such as baggy tops or pants or more androgynous attire
- Changes in underwear choices, which no one else sees

129

- Use of a nickname that is not gendered
- Changes in name or pronouns or use of a nickname
- Use of a sports bra or binder for natal females
- Part-time changes in outward clothing that is less androgynous and more typical of the other gender (this might be done privately, after school, in one's room or home)
- Full-time changes in outward clothing that is more typical of the other gender (this would be done publicly)

These are fully reversible steps that a person might try, evaluate how helpful they are, and then continue to incorporate or look at other possible plateaus.

Your teenager has likely already been trying some of the steps I noted above. That's what happens: through trial and error, they learn what helps them to manage dysphoria. You may not even be aware that what they have been doing (for example, a particular haircut or hairstyle) was an attempt to mitigate dysphoric feelings. This could be a good, productive conversation to have with your teen—it might be an opportunity to learn more about how long they have had these experiences of their gender, how they have tried to respond, what has been helpful, and so on. I'd advise not taking an investigative tone here, as if you're on a mission to find a "fix" for your child's dysphoria. Instead, demonstrate curiosity and openness to the ways your teen has already been trying to respond creatively to what they have been experiencing.

As a parent you may wonder whether it's theologically acceptable for a person to intentionally dress androgynously or use a different name/pronouns. These are questions I do want you to grapple with, and finding good dialogue partners for this will be important. I urge you to see in your child the ways in which they reflect God's image, may feel distress, and are trying to manage that distress, even if the steps they are considering raise more questions for you than answers at the moment.

There are, of course, other steps beyond the ones I've listed above that are available today: the use of hormone blockers, the use of low-dose cross-sex hormones, the use of hormones at a clinical dose, various surgical procedures, and so on. Your teen may be making statements about wanting to take these steps. This is not an uncommon request, although it is not done as often as many teens think. Rather than react to these requests in the moment they're made, you can let your child know that you are interested in what their journey has been like up to today. Learn more about the steps they've tried to take over the past several weeks, months, or even years.

It's usually not helpful at first to focus on partially reversible or irreversible plateaus. Instead, create the kind of relationship with your teen that allows them to feel safe enough to open up with you about what their experience has been like. If your teen hasn't thought about any possible responses to their dysphoria other than medical intervention,[5] it may be helpful to think through other possibilities with them. But this should not be the focus of your initial conversation with them, especially since it may be born primarily out of future-oriented fears rather than a here-and-now presence with your child.

Bringing It Home

Can you imagine yourself having this conversation with your son or daughter? In an interview with a mother of two boys, we discussed what she would want to communicate to either of her sons if he were to experience gender dysphoria or otherwise have questions about his gender identity:

> Wanting to protect my child. Knowing if they struggle with gender identity, the road ahead is not easy. Wanting to protect

them from that. If you are wrestling with those questions or struggling with identity, the safest road of wanting to hide is not how I want to relate in my relationship with my son. Ultimately, there is love and acceptance from me. I want to walk with him through it. There will be decisions he'll have to make throughout a lifetime; I'd like him to do that in partnership with God, and I'd like to find a way to talk about that.

You can see her desire to provide protection for the long journey that is ahead for her son. She is able to acknowledge that the journey will be fraught, and she wants to convey love, acceptance, and a willingness to join him on that journey. Because she knows he will be facing difficult decisions at various points in his life, she wants to stay in the kind of relationship with her son that will allow her to be viewed as a resource. She would love for God to be a resource too, if at all possible.

Let's take a look at how an exchange between a parent and child might look when discussing the child's experience of gender dysphoria or a diverse gender identity:

Parent: I just want to thank you again for sharing with Dad and me about your experience of your gender. It's been a lot to take in, but I'd rather we know and are able to support you and hear more about what you experience than be left in the dark.

Child: Yeah, you're welcome. I wasn't sure how that was going to go, but you've seemed cool about it. I'm not always sure about Dad, but I know you guys love me and will support me. What did you think about the article I sent you on hormone treatment?

Parent: We've both read it and found it really interesting. I'd like to hear more about what you find compelling about certain, specific medical steps like that. Maybe that's something we can take some time this weekend to talk more about.

Child: Sounds good.

Parent: I'd also like to talk with you about seeing someone who specializes in this area of gender. I'm thinking of someone who can hear your experience and what the last several months and years have been like and, taken together, offer their opinion as someone who has seen and provided care to many people who have similar experiences. I think that could be helpful to Dad and me as well.

Child: You mean like a gender clinic where they prescribe hormones?

Parent: There are definitely specialists in clinics who prescribe hormones. What I'm suggesting is not so much an evaluation for whether you are ready for hormones but an assessment about what you have been experiencing, when it began, how it has been over time, even how to best understand it. Then with that understanding, I think we'd be in a better place to hear recommendations for where to go from here.

Child: Well, I know all of that. I can tell you about when it started and what it's been like. I'd just like to move on to what I think I need.

Parent: That makes sense to me. This step I'm suggesting is maybe more for Dad and me. You might also learn some things you had questions about. But even if you didn't learn anything new, it could really help Dad and me understand things better. And I'm sure there are

things you could tell us. We'd love to hear more
from you about what this has been like.

Child: Yeah, I think I can do that. I just don't want to
be asked a ton of questions.

Parent: I can't promise we won't have questions, but
we will try to ask them in a way that doesn't
drive you up a wall. That may be another reason to meet with a specialist. I just think it can
be good to have someone in the room who has
worked with families like ours and who can
help us understand and talk about it in ways
that might head off unnecessary conflict.

Child: So, we'd be left with just necessary conflict?

Parent: Ha! Good one! Yes, something like that.

Cultural Ambassador: Our Three Cs

In this chapter, we have focused on what happens if your child
experiences gender dysphoria. As you apply your convictions
to a situation like this, it's important to consider how you view
the experience of gender dysphoria. We've previously discussed
three lenses through which Christians might view experiences
of gender incongruence. One lens highlights the creation story,
male and female differences, and God's intent for our bodies
and our minds/experiences to align. A ministry emphasis from
this lens has to do with personal sin and its correction. A second
lens recognizes creational intent for male and female but also
acknowledges the reality of the fall. The fall may touch aspects
of human sexuality and gender, making gender discordance
possible for a small percentage of people. A ministry emphasis
from this lens has to do with suffering that befalls people in
a world that is not as it should be. The third lens focuses on
how differences in gender identity reflect an emerging culture
that our society should celebrate. A ministry emphasis from

this lens has to do with navigating a person's sense of self, who they are, and of what community they are a part.

Your convictions will likely be reflected in how you view gender dysphoria. Think through these three lenses and whether one or two of them are particularly compelling to you. Begin to consider why that is. I'd recommend not picking one and rejecting the other two; rather, consider why each is compelling to people in its own way. Are there aspects of all three that could be valuable to the way you approach your child?

Civility comes in as you begin to sort out what you believe and why. You want to hold your beliefs with humility and awareness that not everyone has taken the time to do what you've being doing: slowing down and thinking and praying about what you believe and why. Be gracious and civil toward others, including others in your own family, who are either in that same process or perhaps have skipped the process altogether.

If your child is sharing that they are transgender or that they experience gender dysphoria, lead with compassion. Hold on to your convictions or the process by which you are discerning your convictions; you don't need to abandon them. But for now, lead with compassion. Imagine yourself coming alongside your child or your teen as they are trying to get better footing on a hike with few clear paths to follow. Imagine walking with them. Imagine holding their hand to steady them if they will let you. You are "base camp" on a meaningful journey of identity.[6] Be available. Be present. Ask good questions. When teens do not open up, it's not typically because they don't want to. It is typically because we as parents have asked questions in a way that makes it seem like we already know the answers. Our questions might also reflect fears that we have not worked through just yet. We can make our kids defensive if we approach conversations this way. So don't weaponize your questions. Instead, position yourself emotionally and spiritually alongside your teen as they share with you what they have been experiencing.

PART 4

For the Person Experiencing Gender-Identity Issues

9

What if this is your story?

If you experience your gender in ways that are a departure from what most people experience, I want to thank you for reading this book. Maybe you were genuinely interested in the book, or perhaps someone who loves you asked you to read it. Either way, I'm glad you found your way here, and while you may not agree with everything you read, I hope you have seen the potential value in helping those around you—especially your parents—understand gender identity, transgender experiences, and gender dysphoria. If you've picked up a few insights along the way as well, that's great too.

On the one hand, you may have been told by others that your experience of your gender is just a matter of willful disobedience. As if you made a series of bad choices that brought you to where you are today. Yet you know better, that you did not choose to experience your gender as you do.

You may have been told that you are an abomination. Yet you have read that nothing can separate you from the love of God for you (Romans 8:35–39).

On the other hand, you may have been told that self-actualization comes with medical transitioning. But you know that self-actualization is not an end goal for the Christian. Christlikeness is your end goal, and Christlikeness is the work of the Holy Spirit in you. Transitioning—whether social or medical—is another topic and an important one, so we want to circle back to it later in this chapter.

Our culture is deeply divided on the question of gender. There are those who deny any experience of gender apart from the gender identity that corresponds with a person's biological sex. There are also those who celebrate every possible gender identity as just a part of the diverse gender landscape available to people today. Some people view medical transitioning as a mountaintop experience to which all people with discordant gender identities should aspire.

This polarization leaves little room for a middle ground position. Few people think in terms of middle ground, and fewer know what that path could look like. Before we consider different pathways, it will first be helpful to reflect on your own views of gender identity.

Ways of Seeing Gender Today

How do you view your gender identity? In my previous writing, I have discussed three lenses through which people see gender today. I mentioned these in the last chapter, but I want to go over them again here so you can think about them and reach your own conclusions. You can think of these as ways of understanding your own experience of gender:

- The first lens would say there is a divine, sacred corresponding relationship between biological sex and gender. This understanding would answer gender questions by encouraging correspondence with one's biological sex and view attempts to alter gender and various expressions of diverse gender identities as a moral concern. There is a ministry emphasis on how to avoid *sin* here. Flourishing is found in acquiescence to one's body.

- The second lens would say that there are differences in how gender and gender identity are experienced that signal something is not functioning as it was intended. It would be like having hearing loss, as I mentioned in chapter 3. People with hearing loss are not told today that it is because of sin, or that they are sinning in having hearing loss. In other words, hearing loss is not a moral issue but an issue of function. Something is not functioning properly. Just as a person was meant to experience properly functioning hearing, a person with discordant gender was meant to have their gender and their experience of gender identity correspond to their biological sex. This understanding would answer gender-related questions by helping you manage your dysphoria so that it is not so distressing to you, recognizing that this will vary from person to person and in the same person from time to time. There is a ministry emphasis on how to respond to *suffering* here. Flourishing is growth in Christ amidst enduring hardship.

- The third lens would say that variations in gender and gender identity are a matter of diversity that should be celebrated. This is the most affirming lens to most people navigating gender identity questions. This understanding answers gender-related questions by helping you realize or embody your gender identity as you experience it. There is a ministry emphasis on *self* here and, to some extent, self-actualization. There is an assumption that flourishing is a by-product of self-actualization in how you experience your gender.

Which lens seems to capture where you are in recent weeks or months? Or have you been on a bit of a journey in which you have understood your gender through different lenses at different times? Perhaps there are elements of more than one lens or even all three that resonate with you to one degree or another. That is not uncommon at all. You might reflect on times when different lenses made sense to you—or aspects of different lenses made sense to you. What made that lens seem right to you at the time? How did you move away from that understanding to a different understanding? How did you move toward the lens you currently see gender through?

You may also find that none of the lenses in and of themselves sufficiently captures your experience or answers the questions you have. In my previous writing, I have suggested that each of the three lenses brings something to our discussion. As a result, some people may have a lens that incorporates different aspects of two or even all three of the lenses I described.

For example, I think the biblically faithful starting point is found in the divine or sacred foundations depicted in the stories of creation and the anticipation of gender identity corresponding to one's biological sex. That's the first lens. But I'm less confident that everyone can expect to be restored to creational intent. I have found that gender dysphoria may resolve on its own for many children as they grow up and enter late adolescence, but for others, it continues to be a concern or becomes a concern for the first time later in adolescence or emerging adulthood. In these instances, gender dysphoria is often a more enduring reality. Rather than experiencing creational intent for their gender, some people will experience discomfort—sometimes significant discomfort—that they learn to manage. Management strategies vary considerably

142

and are applied on a case-by-case basis, rather than one approach being intended for all people with similar experiences. This is the second lens. The second lens reminds us that not everything functions as it was intended to function, and while the stories of creation anticipate correspondence, there will be those whose experience does not reflect that ideal scenario. This requires compassion and empathy as we work together to find a way to manage dysphoria.

The last lens, focusing on diversity and a person's sense of self, has as its strength a way of speaking to a person's identity and sense of community. The concept of being transgender or experiencing another gender identity gives a person positive and affirming language for their experience, and a sense of shared identity (or what we think of as community). Instead of simply describing how you are ("I have gender dysphoria"), you can make a more fundamental claim about who you are ("I am transgender"), which many people prefer. Let me also say that there are a number of theologically conservative gender minority people who would say "I am transgender" in a predominantly descriptive way, so it is important to note that not everyone who says "I am transgender" shares the same assumptions about what precisely is involved in a trans identity. While I may not gravitate toward some of the claims made about gender within the mainstream of this lens, I do think this lens reminds us all that we are helping a person navigate their sense of self and have to find language for identity and a way of building community for people who experience a discordant gender identity.

Taken together, these three lenses can lead us to a kind of integrated lens that reflects the best of what each of the lenses offers. You might take some time today and over the next few weeks to jot down which of the lenses resonate with you and why and how that understanding has developed in you over time. How did you come to the place that these aspects of the lenses made the most sense out of what you are experiencing today? How do you wish to address questions that arise from others or even for yourself related to avoidance of *sin*, a response to *suffering*, and navigating your sense of *self*?

Pushing Back against Unhelpful Assumptions

In my work with people navigating gender identity and faith, I am often validating the reality of their gender dysphoria or discordant gender identity. I push back against those who say it isn't real, and I push back against those who say the experience itself is willful disobedience.

But I also push back against those who contribute to a cultural message that medical transitions are a kind of mountaintop experience for those with a discordant gender identity. The medical mountaintop is rarely stated directly, but entertainment and media depictions of such stories communicate a set of assumptions and exclude stories of other life trajectories.

As it turns out, even in this current cultural moment, most adults elect not to medically transition. Fewer than half of adults use hormone treatment and only one in four use any kind of surgical intervention. So the medical mountaintop may be an illusion; most people find a plateau somewhere along the journey. My questions to you are these: what is your plateau, and what kind of support do you need where you are?

Plateaus take many forms. For some people, a plateau is a partial social transition. For others, it is a complete social transition. Still others plateau with some minimal cross-dressing behavior after school or work or only on the weekends. Some people will dress full time in more androgynous attire, while others present as their biological sex but create a social media presence as another gender identity. Still others stay closely aligned with their biological sex because of personal or religious convictions. There may be nearly as many plateaus as there are people plateauing.

So, what is your current plateau? Can you name it and reflect some on how it is going for you? It may also be helpful to reflect on past plateaus or steps you took to manage your dysphoria before you got to where you are today. What have you been doing and how has that been for you? What are you currently doing and how is it going? Keep in mind that a plateau may or may not be a lifelong location. Some plateaus last for four months, while other plateaus last for four years. Or fourteen years. It just depends.

Support

What kind of support are you looking for today? What are you looking for that you aren't getting from the people around you?

You could divide potential support into different groups, such as your immediate family, your extended family, close friends, friends, people at church, your small group from church, your youth group leader, your youth group peers, classmates at school, teachers and other staff at school, and so on.

Be realistic in this exercise. If you know your parents are (or would be) sorting out their response from a Christian world-view or a set of beliefs and values that may not support a full-throated affirmation of specific steps you are considering—such as a complete social transition or a medical transition—what are realistic expectations for support they could show within the framework they adhere to today? If they were to be more supportive but not make a dramatic shift in their views, what would that support look like?

Try to make a broad and long list of people and places where you do things—like home, school, church, etc.—and then reflect on current support you experience and how it is expressed. Try to be really concrete and specific: "I have felt support from my mom when she asks me how I'm doing and just checks in on me from time to time," or "I've felt support when my close friend at school, Jaime, says nice things about what I'm wearing and how I look that day and just seems to find ways to affirm me in ways that matter to me."

Social Media and Culture

We would be remiss not to discuss your experience with social media and how being a part of culture today can affect you. This includes turning to social media as a potential avenue for social support. Daryl, a sixteen-year-old natal male, came to see us for a consultation. He had experienced himself as a girl for the past five to six years and had only recently been able to articulate that and share his experience with his parents and a few close friends. In some regards, Daryl has taken zero steps in making a social transition. In other ways, he is living two lives. He has launched a secret account on a popular social media platform that his parents and friends don't know about. On that account he goes by Deana and presents as a girl. He lives in some fear that people he knows in real life will find that account and share it with others and that he will be "outed" for his transgender identity and gender expression. When he talks to us about it, his persona on this account seems to be an outlet that helps him manage his dysphoria, but the model of compartmentalizing his expressions of self, hiding from others, and living in fear of social consequences in discovery is not sustainable and seems to be taking a toll on his mental health and well-being.

Related to social media presence is the question of how someone like Daryl first connected to others online in a culture that provides him with the language and categories for gender that he has been engaging for several years. A young person's experiences online can lead to powerfully influential interactions with an essentially unfiltered online community. Social media and the culture created therein can shape young minds. It would be helpful to take a balanced look at your own exposure to social media and the culture you've been a part of online. What were some of your earliest experiences online and with social media around gender and sexuality? What are some of the cultural messages surrounding gender, gender identity, and gender expression that you have heard? How have you gone about becoming a critical consumer of that culture? What have you weighed in your mind and said no to? What has been internalized and is true? What has been internalized and may not be true? Do you have people in your life you could discuss this with and perhaps together critically evaluate media and culture? These could be mentors and trusted adults who could help you think through language and categories for gender and assumptions about how best to thrive. Perhaps being able to do this with a trusted mentor who can bring a faith perspective into the conversation will also be helpful to you.

Another more abstract consideration has to do with a broader cultural cynicism toward sources of authority. There are many institutions that have functioned as sources of authority that have come under greater scrutiny recently. Some institutions that have been thought of as tried and true are today viewed more suspiciously; sometimes this has been warranted due to abuse of power. I'm specifically thinking of government officials or even the media, both of which are viewed today with increasing distrust. If we extend our gaze to the church, which is another institution, we see similar concerns. The church is a source of authority that teaches norms about sexuality and gender. There have been some high-profile pastors who have used their power in ways that have hurt the most vulnerable. If institutions are being questioned, the church is one more institution that comes under scrutiny, particularly when the church attempts to teach norms about sexuality and gender.

The norms around sex and gender are also called into question. Not only do the widely diverse experiences of sexuality and gender today contradict what many of us have been told in the past, but the norms for sexuality (attraction to the opposite sex) and gender (concordance between one's gender identity and biological markers) are today viewed as a source of oppression for those whose experiences differ from those norms. It is important to consider how you navigate the norms themselves, the cultural cynicism toward those norms, and the people like yourself who embody alternatives to those norms.

Perhaps take a few moments to reflect on these three questions:

1. How do you navigate (make sense of and respond to) the norms for sexuality and gender themselves?

2. How do you navigate (make sense of and respond to) the cultural cynicism and distrust expressed toward those norms?

3. How do you understand and relate to people who in some ways embody alternatives to those norms?

Social media continues to be a significant influence and source of support to people navigating gender identity in our culture. It can be helpful to reflect on how you experience and navigate social media so that you can be intentional about what you gain from those interactions.

Medical Advances

Another cultural development has to do with medicine. We now have advances in medicine that allow people to do creative, innovative things we could not do previously. Blocking a child from going into puberty is not something we've always been able to do. Offering a teenager cross-sex hormones is not something we've always been able to do. In fact, hormone blockers were originally introduced as a treatment in response to precocious or early puberty, which happens in some instances for largely unknown reasons.[1]

Pediatric endocrinologist Norman Spack introduced hormone blockers in the U.S. as an intervention for youth diagnosed with gender dysphoria in 2007.[2] Hormone blockers had been used for these purposes for years before that in the Netherlands, but in terms of their first use in the U.S., it has been a relatively recent introduction. The use of blockers allows people to push a pause button on puberty and can allow an older child/early adolescent additional time to explore gender identity and for parents to come to a better understanding of the challenges their child and their family are facing. A child/early teen could discontinue the use of blockers and go through puberty as they would have prior to the introduction of blockers; alternatively, a teen could be prescribed cross-sex hormones and medically move in the direction of the gender they experience.

My main point here is to invite you to think deeply and well about medical advances in this area. In other words, the question that comes up is whether we should do creative and innovative things. Many people do not have a framework for that kind of decision-making apart from utility—does it work?

One of the related cultural challenges today is that there is a great push to move gender identity questions out of a mental health framework (i.e., diagnosis of Gender Dysphoria) toward a diversity understanding in which we celebrate differences in gender identity. The questions you may be facing appear to be moving away from the mental health category.

This isn't too surprising. Most people don't want to think of themselves as having something not aligning in the way it was supposed to. People want to be celebrated.

The challenge for the Christian is that we aren't called to simply celebrate who we are.[3] That's not the frame of reference Christians usually use. What we celebrate is what God has done for us. This brings us to a brief reflection on our faith journey.

Faith Journey

Earlier in this chapter, I mentioned the potential value of sorting out social media and cultural messages with a trusted adult, perhaps a mature mentor who is also a Christian. This brings up the topic of your own faith journey, which we want to discuss here.

If you are a Christian, what has it been like for you in your faith journey? Many people I meet with were raised in a Christian home or have been part of a local Christian church. They have often wrestled with how to understand the relationship between their faith and their experience of their gender.

Reflect on your experiences at church and in your youth group or small group as you've walked out your faith journey in community. How have those experiences enriched your faith? In what ways have your experiences placed a greater strain on your walk with Christ?

I'd also like to invite you to reflect on your personal faith and the times when you feel closer to God, as well as the times when you feel more distant. Some people feel closer to God when they are used by him in meaningful service to others. Some people feel closer to God when they spend time reflecting in gratitude on the blessings he has given them.

What has it meant so far to trust that God is a good and loving Father whose plan for your gender is better than the plans laid out for you by those in the world around you?

So far, I have been discussing your personal spiritual journey. A norm for Christians throughout history has been to meet regularly with other believers rather than attempt to grow in Christ on our own. This can be very challenging as you navigate gender identity. A young adult shared with us in a recent gender consultation that they left the church after seeing others treated badly: "I felt really uncomfortable about the way that transgender folks in the church were being treated behind their backs and haven't really been involved in a church since then."

I don't know all of what happened in this instance, but what are you looking for from a local church?

One thing that can be difficult in church and youth group environments is how they are structured. They are often structured around male/female differences that may emphasize stereotypes. For many people, such stereotyping exacerbates existing gender dysphoria and can be especially painful. This will lead some youth to pull away from potential resources in their local church. This pulling away may be necessary at times. However, I want to encourage you to consider whether there is an adult you could talk to about showing greater sensitivity in structuring youth environments for people like you. This might include reducing the number of times the youth group breaks out into boy/girl discussion groups, or offering a single stall bathroom to those for whom the question of which is the appropriate bathroom is more complicated or could be misunderstood by others.

My experience has been that most youth ask important and deep spiritual questions. These can include, "What does God think about me?" This question can be especially heightened in a culture where so much about gender and religion is politicized and spoken of solely in "culture war" terms. What I mean by this is that when you hear disparaging remarks like, "This transgender thing is just one more sign that our nation is going down the toilet!" you end up with a sense that it is an us versus them kind of topic, and you may not know where to turn with the questions you have about your gender and your faith.

Other common questions often asked by people about their youth group, young adult ministry, or larger church include, "Do I belong?" and "Am I wanted here?" I would love for you to be a part of a church, young adult ministry, or youth group that offers a resounding "Yes!" to these two questions—so that you know there is no other place people in your church would rather have you be than part of the church community. I'd love for you to know that God loves you as you are and wants to draw you closer to him, and that one of the main ways we do that is by being a part of a local church.

Expand Your Capacity for Virtues

As an extension of your faith journey, I'd like to encourage you to focus on enjoying and growing in your relationship with Jesus. Much of that relationship is in accord with the work of the Holy Spirit in your life. Perhaps consider the daily, weekly, monthly, and yearly habits that deepen your relationship with Jesus. Toward that end, you can pray that God would be at work in you, expanding your capacity for virtues like faith (trusting in God's guidance and provision for you when it is not immediately obvious to you), hope (believing that good will shine through eventually), charity (selflessly engaging others for their good), temperance (a measured way of going through life, self-control), fortitude (enduring through challenging times), and so on.

I think this can be a better approach than focusing narrowly on your gender and trying to "resolve it" or get it "worked out." Growth in virtues may very well inform decisions you will be facing in the months or years ahead, just as growth in your relationship with Jesus through the work of the Holy Spirit will also inform decisions you may be facing.

As you pray to expand your capacity for these various virtues, you may find you reframe many of the day-to-day exchanges you have with people, including your parents. Perhaps rather than feel exasperated by how slowly they seem to be grasping what you are sharing, you can begin to see this as an opportunity to grow in patience. You can pray for more peace (freedom from disturbance and a calmness of mind and spirit) and for the capacity for patience as you wait on God's plan, will, and timing.

Bringing It Home

Let's flip the dialogue here and focus on what you would say to your parents. In my observation, many younger people find aspects of the diversity lens appealing. They like the focus on identity and community, of being a part of the transgender community and the broader LGBTQ+ community. It has sometimes brought them a much-needed sense of solidarity with others that they have not found at home or in their local church or broader faith circle.

I can imagine several conversations you might have with your parents about what you experience. Many parents want to improve their relationship with their child, but they don't know how. Parents and kids can wind up speaking past each other, or a parent's anxiety and fears can drive the conversation in ways that exasperate their teen.

> Child: I'd like to find a way for us to talk about what my gender has been like for me.
>
> Parent: I'd like to find a way for us to talk about what you've been going through too.

Child: I'm not sure how to describe it, but ever since I was very young, I haven't felt right in my body. It's a hard thing to talk about, in part because I don't know what it would feel like for my body to feel right to me. I just know it hasn't felt right, and it hasn't felt right for a long time.

Parent: What do you mean when you say you don't feel right in your body? I'm not sure I understand what that means.

Child: I know that probably sounds crazy, but it's true. I look around at my friends, other people I know, you and Dad, and it just seems like they are comfortable in their bodies. They seem to be doing fine. But I don't feel that way. I'm not sure if I've ever felt that way. I just never knew how to talk about it. I didn't know what it meant.

Parent: Are you saying you know now what it means? It makes sense now? What do you think it means?

Child: I think it means my gender doesn't line up with my sex. Like, I know that my sex has to do with my biology, but my gender doesn't seem to match it. When I first heard someone use the word *transgender*, I realized that that might be me. I didn't even know that it was possible, but it makes sense to me now and seems to be what I'm like. It seems to be who I am.

Parent: What makes you think it seems to be who you are?

Child: Because when people describe transgender, they are describing a person whose gender is, like, the other gender. A boy who experiences himself as a girl or vice versa. That's what I've felt like, but I've never had a name for it.

This dialogue reflects a way to describe what you experience to your parents without jumping into identity categories too quickly or in ways that might feel antagonistic to your parents. Recall that your parents likely see this topic through a different lens than you do, a lens that they might not have had an opportunity to reflect on. You are describing your experience using words that make more sense to your parents. Being more descriptive about your gender identity and experience may be helpful in communication.

Cultural Ambassador: Our Three Cs

I'd like to close this chapter by talking about how to apply the three Cs to your own life and experience. I didn't introduce you to the three lenses so you would feel forced to pick one, as though the complex questions you have would be answered once and for all. Rather, I was hoping to introduce you to a wide range of ways people have thought about the topic, including people like you, who experience their gender identity like you do.

We are meaning-making creatures whose search for meaning can lead us in all sorts of directions. It can be helpful to reflect on those different directions, read up on other people's experiences, pray about this, and discuss it with others. This will, over time, bring you to a place of some conviction. In my view, it can be helpful to think about your bigger-picture convictions too: the claims of Christianity, the authority of Scripture, what Christians have written about and thought about sexuality and gender through the ages, and what Christians are saying today. You might want to read examples of people who experience their gender in ways you experience your gender and expand your own sense of which paths people have gone down.

You can grow in broader convictions about your faith, about what is true, about sources of authority, and about the virtues you want to see develop in you over time. You can also grow in convictions about gender, gender identity, and gender expression.

As you develop your convictions, you can also learn to relate to others, including your parents or friends or people in your youth group, out of a place of civility. There will be people in your life who will force you to decide if you can agree to disagree with them, even on topics that are very important to you.

Compassion toward yourself and toward others is our third commitment. If you struggle with self-compassion or extending grace to yourself, you might find it helpful to role-play how you would respond to your best friend if they were experiencing what you experience. What would you say to them? How would you want to come alongside them and be a source of support to them? Can you find a way to extend the same compassion or grace you show to your friend to yourself?

Compassion can also be extended toward others. I'm thinking here especially of your parents. They may not understand your experiences, or perhaps they have responded poorly to you. I am not exonerating them for any wrongdoing. I am suggesting that they too are on a journey as they take in new information about what you have been experiencing. They may have had a lot of unhelpful assumptions about gender and gender identity that make talking with you that much harder. They have their own lens through which they see the topic—and that lens has developed over time. It could be helpful to come to a better understanding of that lens, how it developed for them, and why it is compelling, just as you might want them to understand how you see things, which lens resonates with you, and how that lens came to resonate with you over time.

Afterword

This book was meant primarily for Christian parents. It was meant to prepare you to have better conversations with your kids about an important cultural moment centered on sex and gender. Many Christian parents are struggling to sort out what they believe about gender identity, transgender experiences, and emerging gender identities. They don't know how to respond to the proliferation of gender identities that their children are learning in school and online. They are especially struggling to find the right words and tone for their conversations with their children and teens.

I hope this book will in some small way add to your expanding resources as you prepare to talk with your children about this important topic. I hope you've found in this book an angle of entry into this topic, giving you language to navigate a conversation you may have been avoiding or hoping would go away.

The dialogues throughout this book may not sound like you. That's okay. When I was initially training to be a counselor, I observed my supervisor in session. She had a wonderful way of being present with people and phrasing things. What I said to my clients never seemed to be as good as what she said. She would often say during supervision, "Borrow my language." I would borrow her language in the next session. What I said didn't initially sound like me, but I eventually found my voice, and today much of what I say is a reflection of my various supervisors and how I would say what I have learned in a voice that is finally my own. As you review the dialogues in the book, try to take the spirit of what was said and make it your own. Try to find your voice. If that's hard, consider borrowing my language until you find your voice in how you want to talk to your kids about gender and gender identity.

It's also okay if you don't get it right every time. Most parents have wished they had said something different or had a different tone or posture when addressing topics that are difficult to talk about. You may have had fears that were especially heightened at one time that have since been allayed. If you've misspoken or said something in a tone you regret, you can revisit that conversation, apologize, and take another turn communicating what's on your heart and mind.

We want to avoid the "culture warrior" posture that could lead our children to think we hate their friends and classmates. We also want to avoid becoming the "cultural capitulator" who seems to act as though Christianity has nothing to say about these important topics or is utterly irrelevant to the present moment. I hope you'll seek instead to become a "cultural ambassador." You are an ambassador of one kingdom to the broader culture around you. Your children grow up in your home, where you provide foundational knowledge, beliefs, and values,[1] while they simultaneously grow up in a broader cultural context with all of the messages embedded therein. They are learning from you how to be cultural ambassadors of their own Christian faith over time. They will need to discern truth for themselves and make choices about how they convey that truth. As I noted in the preface, you can cut with the sword of truth or you can point with the sword of truth. This book is intended to help you take a pointing approach in the context of a sustained presence in the lives of others.

In ambassadorship, we aim for *convicted civility seasoned with compassion*. The three Cs can be a great way to guide your thinking and your exchanges with your kids in the years to come. There is a balance there that is hard to attain but can be very rewarding, especially as your kids look to you to help them understand how the faith they were raised in has any bearing on the present moment. It does, and the way you hold on to and display that faith will go far in helping them come to that realization. There may be times when our kids do not come to that same realization; sometimes the conclusions we draw from our faith do not *necessarily* translate into our children's conclusions. There is value in reaching your own conclusions, even (and especially) if you feel like your kids won't see things in quite the same way you do. If you find yourself having a hard time striking the right balance, be patient with yourself, find good people to process that struggle with, ask God for help, and keep at it. You can do it.

Acknowledgments

No one I know does research all by themselves. We are part of research and scholarship-developing communities. At the Sexual & Gender Identity (SGI) Institute, this includes SGI Fellows Dr. Julia Sadusky, Dr. Janet Dean, Dr. Stephen Stratton, and Dr. Olya Zaporozhets. Current members of SGI are Kevin Biondolillo, Micaela Hardyman, Ethan Martin, Anna Brose, Ruth Fu, Carly Quibodeaux, Mia Menassa, David O'Connor, Ian Sneller, Nathan Palladino, Angela Pak, Christina Claudia, Stephen Jennings, Emily Brabac, and SJ Kim.

With this book, I am especially grateful for people who read through drafts of chapters and provided me with their thoughts and recommendations. This includes Mitch Kim, Lori Yarhouse, and Kelly Arensen. I interviewed several parents about their experiences with their own children, and I am deeply grateful for their willingness to share their experiences with me. I am also grateful to Greg Coles for his careful reading of the manuscript and editorial suggestions throughout. Thank you too to my editors at Bethany House: Andy McGuire, for the conversations we have had that led to this book topic and for his editorial work, and Ellen McAuley, for helping me more clearly communicate what I was wanting to communicate.

A book for Christian parents is also based on years of conversations with parents about the topic of gender identity. Meetings with parents have been through consultations and ongoing counseling services. Research also informs a book like this, as we have been conducting research with Christian parents for more than a decade. When I share an example in the book, the names and any identifying information have been changed to protect anonymity. I want to acknowledge and thank the parents who have invited me in and shared their experiences with me through the years.

Notes

Why This Book Is Important

1. Not too long ago I was providing a training on gender identity to a group of board members who oversee a major Christian institution. After speaking for about an hour, I opened up our time to Q&A, and the first question had to do with how common it is for someone to be transgender. I answered him with the data we had at the time, which suggested it is not that common, and he asked, "So why spend time on this?"

The answer to why we spend time on a topic is not always in direct proportion to the number of people who have an experience, but also in relation to the magnitude of the impact of that topic. Today we are seeing an increase in the number of people—especially younger people—who identify as transgender or nonbinary, but we are also seeing wider changes in how people think about norms related to sexuality and gender. These wider changes mean more and more people will be challenged to reflect on what they believe about gender and why.

2. This framing of Christian engagement draws upon Niebuhr's well-known typology. When I think of "cultural capitulator," this more closely aligns with Niebuhr's Christ of Culture. Similarly, "culture warrior" is closest to Niebuhr's Christ Against Culture. What I am aiming for with "cultural ambassador" is a cultural engagement that is closest to Niebuhr's Christ as Transformer of Culture, which is indebted to the work of Augustine and Calvin. H. Richard Niebuhr, *Christ & Culture* (New York: Harper & Row, 1975).

3. The language of "convicted civility" has been attributed to Richard Mouw, who has attributed it to Martin Marty. I added "seasoned with compassion" to complement the commitment by Mouw and Marty to hold convictions and civility together, as critical dimensions of relating to others

around polarizing topics. *Compassion* reminds me that the topics themselves are reflected in the lives of real people.

4. Anne Lamott, *Bird by Bird: Some Instructions on Writing and Life* (New York: Anchor Books, 2007), 156. The context of this quote was Lamott's interactions with someone in a writing group who had provided rather abrasive feedback to another member of the group.

Chapter 1 Why are transgender experiences suddenly so prominent?

1. All names are pseudonyms to protect anonymity.

2. The estimates cited there are in the range of 0.005% to 0.014% of adult men and 0.002% to 0.003% of adult women. See American Psychiatric Association, *Diagnostic and Statistical Manual of Mental Disorders*, 5th ed., 454.

3. See the report and summary of the 2015 U.S. Transgender Survey at https://transequality.org/sites/default/files/docs/usts/USTS-Full-Report -Dec17.pdf.

4. For example, the Williams Institute at UCLA reported that 0.6% of the adult population identify as transgender. They then estimated using a modeling strategy that there would be differences by race and ethnicity, and suggested that 0.8% of adults who are African-American or Black, 0.8% of adults who are Latino or Hispanic, 0.6% of adults who are of another race or ethnicity, and 0.5% of White adults identify as transgender.

Similarly, Kenneth Zucker reported a range between 0.5% and 1.3% for children, adolescents, and adults who experience either gender dysphoria or have a transgender identity. See K. J. Zucker, "Epidemiology of Gender Dysphoria and Transgender Identity," Sexual Health 14 (2017): 404–11.

5. Information on the recent Gallup Poll can be accessed here: Jeffrey M. Jones, "LGBT Identification in U.S. Ticks Up to 7.1%," Gallup, February 17, 2022, https://news.gallup.com/poll/389792/lgbt-identification-ticks-up .aspx.

6. "Social contagion," APA Dictionary of Psychology, https://dictionary .apa.org/social-contagion.

7. See Stephen Allison, Megan Warin, and Tarun Bastiampillai, "Anorexia Nervosa and Social Contagion: Clinical Implications," *Australian and New Zealand Journal of Psychiatry* 48, no. 2 (2014): 116–20.

8. See Mark Yarhouse and Julia Sadusky, *Emerging Gender Identities: Understanding the Diverse Experiences of Today's Youth* (Grand Rapids, MI: Brazos Press, 2020).

9. Ian Hacking refers to this effect, which we describe in greater detail and apply to the experience of gender dysphoria in Mark Yarhouse and Julia Sadusky, *Emerging Gender Identities*, 27–43.

Chapter 2 What causes someone to experience gender dysphoria?

1. https://transequality.org/sites/default/files/docs/usts/USTS-Full-Report -Dec17.pdf. In the report, 32% of adults reported first gender discordance

under the age of 5, 28% between the ages of 6 and 10, whereas 21% reported onset between ages 11 and 15, 13% between the ages of 16 and 20, and 6% ages 21 and older.

2. The rise in the number of late-onset cases among adolescent females in particular has led some to connect this to the concept of "social contagion," which I mentioned in chapter 1. Proponents of this view cite studies of social contagion as a pathway to eating disorders among adolescent females and see the rise in cases of gender dysphoria as analogous.

Chapter 3 What does the Bible say about being transgender?

1. For example, Peter Craigie writes:
    Again, although the precise reason for the prohibition is uncertain, it may have been related to some custom practiced in Egypt. The word *sha*ʿ*aṭnēz*, which is not Hebrew, appears to be a word taken over from Egyptian; this may indicate that the reason for the prohibition is to be found in Egypt. It may be noted that during the Eighteenth Dynasty, various complicated types of pattern weaves were being introduced in Egypt, perhaps from Syria, and they may therefore have had reprehensible associations (no longer known) for the Israelites.
Peter Craigie, *The Book of Deuteronomy* (NICOT; Grand Rapids, MI: Eerdmans, 1976), 291.

2. See *Transsexuality: A Report by the Evangelical Alliance Policy Commission* (Reading, UK: Cox & Wyman, 2000), 47: "The cross-dressing prohibition was introduced to prevent involvement on the part of the Israelites in contemporary Canaanite religious rituals of the day, which involved swapping of sex roles and cross-dressing." On the one hand are concerns about idolatry and pagan practices, while another interpretation of Deuteronomy 22:5 is that it may have to do with "preserving the order built into creation, specifically the fundamental distinction between male and female," Daniel I. Block, *Deuteronomy: The NIV Application Commentary* (Grand Rapids, MI: Zondervan, 2012), 512.

3. This is a paraphrase of a colleague of mine at Wheaton College, Dr. John Walton, who has said that a passage was not written *to* you, rather, it was written *for* you.

4. Mark A. Yarhouse and Erica S. N. Tan, *Sexuality and Sex Therapy: A Comprehensive Christian Appraisal* (Downers Grove, IL: InterVarsity Press Academic, 2014), 25–27.

5. Oscar Cullmann, *Christ and Time, 3rd Edition* (London: SCM Press, 2018), 84.

6. Thank you to Mitchel Kim for his thoughts on Romans 8:19–22 and for connecting these reflections to the statement on sexuality from the Christian and Missionary Alliance that says, "Because of the fall, our struggles with sexuality cannot simply be reduced to our choices or environmental background, but our choices remain significant."

7. We were not meant to experience a stroke or heart attack or infection or disease. Nor were we meant to experience depression or anxiety. Although each of these conditions is unique and there may be ways a person makes decisions that indirectly contribute to a specific health or mental health outcome, these concerns are broadly considered nonmoral realities that exist in a fallen world. We respond to them with compassion.

8. It should be noted that people view hearing loss differently. Some view hearing loss as a disability or medical condition, while others view hearing loss as reflecting a unique culture to be celebrated.

9. Heather Looy, "Male and Female God Created Them: The Challenge of Intersexuality," *Journal of Psychology and Christianity* 21, no. 1 (2002): 17.

Chapter 4 What do I tell my child about gender in general?

1. Carl Gold, "The Intersex Spectrum," Nova, October 29, 2001, www.pbs.org/wgbh/nova/article/intersex-spectrum.

2. Although different cultures throughout history have had different terms for these kinds of experiences, I think something like this has been present to one degree or another in different cultures and societies.

3. Mark Yarhouse and Julia Sadusky, *Emerging Gender Identities*, 21–43.

4. One of the most comprehensive resources on discussing sex with your children is from Stan Jones and Brenna Jones: *How and When to Tell Your Kids about Sex*. Their book is for parents to read and understand the basic approach they recommend as parents raise their kids and provide the kind of framework I have described. The GOD'S DESIGN FOR SEX series that accompanies their book is especially helpful. Wisely, Jones and Jones offer suggestions for talking about sex from a developmental standpoint: a book for children ages 3–5 (*The Story of Me*); ages 5–8 (*Before I Was Born*); ages 8–12 (*What's the Big Deal?*); and ages 12–16 (*Facing the Facts*).

5. Tracy E. Gilchrist, "Pantene Features Trans Child with Lesbian Moms in Heartwarming Ad," Advocate, March 22, 2021, www.advocate.com/transgender/2021/3/22/pantene-features-trans-child-lesbian-moms-heartwarming-ad.

6. Bill Brioux, "Transgender participant is an *Amazing Race* first," *Toronto Star*, July 2, 2015, www.thestar.com/entertainment/television/2015/07/02/transgender-participant-is-an-amazing-race-first.html.

Chapter 5 What do I say when my child asks about someone in their class who has decided to transition?

1. This is in large part because in what is referred to as the Dutch model (developed at the Free University of Amsterdam), the emphasis on comprehensive mental health evaluations alongside evaluations of gender dysphoria led to fewer children being thought of as good candidates for puberty blocking. Most of these children have ended up using cross-sex hormones, but supports would argue that they were probably better candidates for such medical

intervention than children who do not go through a more comprehensive assessment. See Alex Bakker, *The Dutch Approach: Fifty Years of Transgender Health Care at the VU Amsterdam Gender Clinic* (Amsterdam, Netherlands: Boom, 2021), 157–164.

2. See Mark A. Yarhouse, *Understanding Gender Dysphoria: Navigating Transgender Issues in a Changing Culture* (Downers Grove, IL: InterVarsity Press Academic, 2015), 123–24.

Chapter 6 How should I guide my child in their interactions with a transgender friend?

1. Anne Lamott, *Bird by Bird*.

Chapter 7 Are there any early signs that my child may be struggling with gender dysphoria?

1. "What is Gender Dysphoria?" American Psychiatric Association, August 2022, www.psychiatry.org/patients-families/gender-dysphoria/what-is-gender-dysphoria.

2. "What is Gender Dysphoria?" American Psychiatric Association.

3. In a small study we conducted on Christians navigating gender identity at Christian colleges, we reported that twelve of the thirty-one transgender students (38.7%) surveyed indicated that they had attempted suicide. This is much higher than what you would see reported in a sample of U.S. college students, where, in a recent study, 9.3% of students indicated a past suicide attempt. But it is similar to what has been reported among transgender students (38.2%) at public institutions of higher education. See Mark Yarhouse, Janet Dean, Stephen Stratton, Heather Keefe, and Michael Lastoria, "Listening to Transgender and Gender Diverse Students on Christian College Campuses," *Journal of Religion and Health* 60 (2021): 4480–99; C. H. Liu, C. Stevens, S. H. M. Wong, M. Yasui, and J. A. Chen, Note: "The Prevalence and Predictors of Mental Health Diagnoses and Suicide among U.S. College Students: Implications for Addressing Disparities in Service Use," *Depression and Anxiety* 36, no.1 (2019): 8–17.

4. We discuss this as parental scaffolding in Mark A. Yarhouse and Julia A. Sadusky, *Gender Identity and Faith* (Downers Grove, IL: InterVarsity Press Academic, 2022).

Chapter 8 How can I help my child who is struggling with dysphoria?

1. This case was presented in greater detail in Yarhouse and Sadusky, *Gender Identity and Faith*, 61–63.

2. See Yarhouse and Sadusky, *Gender Identity and Faith*, 53–64.

3. Indeed, the UK and some European nations have taken steps to reevaluate medical interventions with minors. I think some professionals are realizing that the model of care that utilizes medical interventions such as

puberty blockers and hormone therapy was developed in a specific gender clinic in the Netherlands (this is the Dutch model), where there was more comprehensive assessment. The concerns parents and others may be voicing have to do with efforts to incorporate elements of that approach without the corresponding comprehensive assessment of both gender dysphoria and co-occurring concerns. There are several places in the eighth edition of the World Professional Association for Transgender Health's Standards of Care that highlight the Dutch model and its comprehensiveness with children in particular.

4. The "gender train" analogy is from Dr. Laura Edwards-Leeper.

5. In a recent survey of over 28,000 transgender adults, plateaus reported include medical interventions such as gender confirmation surgeries (25%) and hormone treatment (44%). But other plateaus included use of different pronouns (84%), making a social transition (62%), presenting as neither a man nor a woman (21%), and living part-time in one gender (15%). See S. E. James et al., *The Report of the 2015 U.S. Transgender Survey* (Washington, D.C.: National Center for Transgender Equality, 2016), (99, 100, 49, 47), www.ustranssurvey.org/reports.

6. This is a metaphor we develop in more detail in *Understanding Sexual Identity*, and it can be adapted for a journey around gender identity and faith. See Mark A. Yarhouse, *Understanding Sexual Identity* (Grand Rapids, MI: Zondervan, 2013).

Chapter 9 What if this is your story?

1. Boston Children's Hospital, Precocious Early Puberty, www.childrenshospital.org/conditions/precocious-early-puberty#symptoms--causes.

2. Alix Spiegel, "Parents Consider Treatment to Delay Son's Puberty," NPR WBEZ Chicago, May 8, 2008, www.npr.org/templates/story/story.php?storyId=90273278.

3. Let's not conclude that celebration of the way we have been created is a bad thing; as Psalm 139:14 evinces ("I praise you because I am fearfully and wonderfully made"), it is good to celebrate God's intentionality in our creation.

Afterword

1. For a comprehensive model of sex education from a Christian worldview, see Stan and Brenna Jones, *How and When to Tell Your Kids about Sex, 3rd ed.* (Colorado Springs: NavPress, 2019). The corresponding books/booklets in the GOD'S DESIGN FOR SEX series, also by Stan and Brenna Jones, are a helpful complement to the book for parents. These are *The Story of Me*; *Before I Was Born: God Knew My Name*; *What's the Big Deal? Why God Cares about Sex*; and *Facing the Facts: The Truth about Sex and You*.

About the Author

Mark Yarhouse is the Dr. Arthur P. and Mrs. Jean May Rech Professor of Psychology at Wheaton College, where he also directs the Sexual & Gender Identity Institute. An award-winning teacher, psychologist, and researcher, Dr. Yarhouse has authored numerous books and articles, including the featured white paper on sexual identity for the Gospel Coalition's Christ on Campus Initiative. He lives in Winfield, Illinois.